# *Guide to*

## THE

# LONG PATH

Third Edition 1992

NEW YORK-NEW JERSEY TRAIL CONFERENCE 1920

## The New York-New Jersey Trail Conference

Published by

New York-New Jersey Trail Conference
G.P.O. Box 2250
New York, New York 10116

**Library of Congress Cataloging-in-Publication Data**

New York-New Jersey Trail Conference.
  Guide to the Long Path / by the New York-New Jersey Trail
Conference. -- 3rd ed.
    p.   cm.
  ISBN 1-880775-00-X
  1. Hiking--Long Path (N.J. and N.Y.)--Guidebooks.  2. Long Path
Region (N.J. and N.Y.)--Guidebooks.  I. Title.
GV199.42.N52L666  1992      917.47'38--dc20           92-19099 CIP

## PHOTO CREDITS

Cover photographs:

George Washington Bridge and the Palisades,
Michael Warren

Sunrise on the Ashokan Reservoir from Cornell Mountain,
Nick Zungoli

Text photographs:

R.J. Bertko, page 31
David Bieri, pages 89, 95
Daniel Chazin, pages 43, 71, 72, 88, 109, 110, 112, 118, 134, 135
Howard Dash, pages 6, 14, 146
Steve Dundorf, pages 93, 136
Art Fazakas, page 73
Gary Haugland, pages 50, 51, 53, 58
Aaron Schoenberg, pages 25, 83, 128
Michael Warren, page 44
Nick Zungoli, pages xiv, 37

ISBN: 1-880775-00-X

# Table of contents

# Table of distances

| Section | From | To | Miles | Cumulative |
|---|---|---|---|---|
| 1 | George Washington Bridge | Route 9W at Lamont-Doherty | 12.70 | 12.70 |
| 2 | Route 9W at Lamont-Doherty | Nyack (Mountainview Ave.) | 9.95 | 22.65 |
| 3 | Nyack (Mountainview Ave.) | Long Clove (Route 9W) | 8.90 | 31.55 |
| 4 | Long Clove (Route 9W) | Mount Ivy (Route 202) | 6.80 | 38.35 |
| 5 | Mount Ivy (Route 202) | Lake Skannatati (7 Lakes Dr.) | 8.90 | 47.25 |
| 6 | Lake Skannatati (7 Lakes Dr.) | Route 6 (Long Mountain Pkwy.) | 10.15 | 57.40 |
| 7 | Route 6 (Long Mountain Pkwy.) | Woodbury (Route 32) | 11.00 | 68.40 |
| 8 | Woodbury (Route 32) | Salisbury Mills (Route 94) | 9.10 | 77.50 |
| 9 | Salisbury Mills (Route 94) | Rock Tavern (Route 207) | 7.30 | 84.80 |
| 10 | Rock Tavern (Route 207) | Montgomery (Route 17K) | 7.60 | 92.40 |
| 11 | Montgomery (Route 17K) | Ulsterville (Route 52) | 11.20 | 103.60 |
| 12 | Ulsterville (Route 52) | Jenny Lane (Route 44/55) | 16.80 | 120.40 |
| 13 | Jenny Lane (Route 44/55) | Riggsville (Catskill Park) | 12.80 | 133.20 |
| 14 | Riggsville (Catskill Park) | Bull Run | 10.10 | 143.30 |
| 15 | Bull Run | Denning Road | 7.60 | 150.90 |
| 16 | Denning Road | Woodland Valley | 11.15 | 162.05 |
| 17 | Woodland Valley | Phoenicia | 5.75 | 167.80 |
| 18 | Phoenicia | Lake Hill | 11.40 | 179.20 |
| 19 | Lake Hill | Platte Clove Road | 12.50 | 191.70 |
| 20 | Platte Clove Road | Palenville | 10.00 | 201.70 |
| 21 | Palenville | North Lake | 4.80 | 206.50 |
| 22 | North Lake | Batavia Kill | 9.80 | 216.30 |
| 23 | Batavia Kill | Route 23 (East Windham) | 8.55 | 224.85 |
| 24 | Route 23 (East Windham) | Greene County Route 10 | 6.95 | 231.80 |
| 25 | Greene County Route 10 | Greene County Route 32C | 4.50 | 236.30 |

# Preface

Soon after the second edition of the *Guide to the Long Path* appeared in 1987, it became evident that a comprehensive revision of the guide was required. Wayne Richter, then Chairman of the Conference's Conservation Committee, volunteered to produce a new edition of the book. He spent many days remeasuring the Long Path and writing detailed descriptions of the trail, which included much interesting information about vegetation, geology and other natural features along the trail. Unfortunately, before he was able to complete the project, he moved out of the area. We all owe a great debt to Wayne, who is largely responsible for this book.

Howard Dash, our Long Path Chairman, took over where Wayne left off, and wrote descriptions for most of the remaining sections, with the assistance of the supervisors of the respective sections. As Publications Chairman, I edited the book and tried to produce a consistent style.

Thanks are also due to Nancy Lucas, who was responsible for the typesetting and design of the text, and to Steve Butfilowski, who designed the cover.

As is apparent from the introductory material, the Long Path is constantly in a state of flux. During the final editing process, many changes had to be made to account for new relocations, and more relocations are in the process of being built. In addition, it is anticipated that new sections will soon be opened north of the Catskills and along the Shawangunk Ridge. In all cases, hikers should follow the aqua Long Path blazes, even if the route they follow differs from that described in this guide, and should contact the Trail Conference for further information.

*Daniel D. Chazin*
*Publications Chairman*

# Overview of the Long Path

The Long Path begins in Fort Lee, on the New Jersey side of the George Washington Bridge. For the first twelve miles to the New York State line, it follows along the Palisades through lands of the Palisades Interstate Park. There are many spectacular views of the Hudson River and New York City and Yonkers along the way.

After crossing into New York, the Long Path turns away from the Hudson River, but continues to follow the Palisades Escarpment to its end in Mt. Ivy. Much of this route is through units of the Palisades Interstate Park system and county and town parks. However, some of the vital links along the way take the trail through private property, and there is some road walking through the towns of Piermont and Nyack. There are extensive views of the lower Hudson River valley along the way, with the most dramatic views on Hook Mountain and High Tor.

Leaving the Palisades, the Long Path enters Harriman State Park, passing through the park in a northwesterly direction. Since Harriman is only thirty miles from New York City, it is frequented by hikers from the city. The park is criss-crossed with an abundance of trails, and there are many opportunities for circular hikes, using the Long Path for part of the route. Harriman State Park contains a portion of the Ramapo Mountains which, at elevations ranging from 1,000 to 1,400 feet, are the lowest mountains in the Appalachian mountain chain. At the northern end of the park, the Long Path goes over Long Mountain, the site of the Torrey Memorial for Raymond H. Torrey, one of the founders of the Trail Conference and an early supporter of the Long Path.

North of Harriman, the trail descends to the Hudson

Valley. For the next fifty miles, the Long Path largely follows roads through Orange County. Once consisting primarily of farms, this area is rapidly being developed into a bedroom community for New York City. The Long Path follows off-road routes through Orange County only in two sections—Schunemunk Mountain and the abandoned New York, Ontario and Western Railroad right-of-way.

Schunemunk is the dramatic long ridge that is the westernmost mountain near the Hudson in this vicinity. It is made up of conglomerate rock and has spectacular views both east to the Hudson River and north to the Shawangunks and the Catskills.

North of Schunemunk, the trail follows a six-mile section of the abandoned New York, Ontario and Western Railroad right-of-way. The NYO&W was once the main line from New York City to the resorts of the Sullivan County Catskills. With the emerging popularity of the automobile, it fell into hard times and was abandoned in the 1950's—well before the rails-to-trails movement began. The right-of-way has reverted to the private landowners, and there is little evidence of the railroad anymore.

Beyond the Hudson Valley, the Long Path climbs the escarpment of the Shawangunk Mountains. Characterized by beautiful white cliffs and spectacular waterfalls, the Shawangunks are one of the gems of the eastern United States. The Shawangunks are also the site of five mountaintop lakes that are rimmed with white cliffs. The Long Path passes two of these lakes—Mud Pond and Lake Awosting. The trail climbs up and over many of the cliffs and passes two of the waterfalls—Verkeerder Kill and Rainbow Falls. There are many spectacular views of the Hudson Valley and the Catskills, sometimes with Lake Awosting in the foreground.

Beyond the Shawangunks, the Long Path crosses the Rondout Valley entirely on roads. To date, this rural area has avoided the development pressures that have hit the Hudson Valley.

At the west end of the Rondout Valley, the Long Path enters the Catskill Park. The Catskills were once thought to be the highest mountains in New York, as they rise abruptly from the Hudson River valley. The Long Path continues through the Catskill Park for 95 miles and goes over nine of the 35 peaks which are over 3,500 feet in elevation. There are many views along the way, and one gets a true sense of wilderness here. Camping is permitted throughout the Catskill Park, except within 150 feet of a trail or stream and in areas over 3,500 feet in elevation, and several lean-tos are located along the Long Path. There are several roadwalking sections, but these are generally through undeveloped areas.

North of the Catskill Park, the trail follows a series of mountains that form a part of the Catskill Mountains. While only about 2,700 to 3,400 feet in elevation, these mountains offer a beautiful hiking experience. About eight miles north of the Catskill Park, the Long Path enters a State reforestation area, which is a working forest (as opposed to the Catskill Park, which must be kept "forever wild"). The Long Path currently ends in the Town of Ashland, about twelve miles north of the Catskill Park. Work continues to extend the trail north to the Mohawk River and the Adirondacks.

# History of the Long Path

The Long Path was originally conceived in the early 1930's by Vincent J. Schaefer of the Mohawk Valley Hiking Club and his brother Paul, who proposed that New York State establish its own "Long Path" similar to the Long Trail in Vermont. Unlike the Long Trail, the Long Path was intended to be an unmarked route through a ten-mile corridor in the backcountry. The challenge of the Long Path was to bushwhack through the corridor using topographical maps. The corridor itself was intended to serve as a link between points of interest. As such, the Long Path was an early example of what today we would call a "greenway."

As originally conceived, the Long Path was to extend from the George Washington Bridge to Whiteface Mountain in the Adirondacks. The route was scouted by W.W. Cady from the George Washington Bridge to Gilboa in the Schoharie Valley, and by Vincent Schaefer from Gilboa to the northern Adirondacks.

The name of the trail came from the weekly column in the *New York Post* by Raymond H. Torrey, one of the authors of the first edition of the *New York Walk Book* and a founder of the New York-New Jersey Trail Conference. His column, "The Long Brown Path," popularized the trail idea. Every week, Torrey would write about a fictional hike along the Long Path.

In 1935, the Palisades Interstate Park Commission began to acquire property for the Palisades Interstate Parkway, and its construction (which increased the accessibility of the Palisades cliffs) renewed interest in the Long Path project. The first section of the Long Path was built along the Palisades in the 1930's. The original proposal was to use the Northville-Lake Placid Trail, built a few years earlier by the Adirondack Mountain Club, as the northern portion of the route. W.W. Cady of New York City assisted in the project south of the Catskills, and some marking was done. However, after a few years, momentum was lost, and the Long Path idea became dormant for over 25 years.

In 1960, Robert Jensen of the Ramapo Ramblers and Michael Warren of New York City urged revival of the project. By 1960, the post-war boom and the growth of suburbia had changed the original concept of the Long Path. Now, the goal was to build a marked footpath from New York City to the Adirondacks. Jensen and others soon began field work between New York City and the Catskills.

The trail was constructed north to the Catskill Park in the 1960's and 1970's. In the Catskills, the Long Path followed existing trails as much as possible. However, new trail construction was needed in certain areas, such as over Peekamoose and Table Mountains. In 1987, the Long Path was finally completed to East Windham, when the "missing link" section around Kaaterskill High Peak was opened. It was now possible to hike continuously the 225 miles from the George Washington Bridge to East Windham at the northern end of the Catskill Park.

In 1985, H. Neil Zimmerman of the Trail Conference began work on extending the Long Path north from the Catskills to the Adirondacks. The plan was to open the first section of the extension as part of the Forest Preserve Centennial celebration. Eight miles of trail were in fact laid out north of East Windham. However, due to difficulties in obtaining permission from landowners, this first section of trail was not opened until 1990. As of the publication of this book (spring 1992), twelve miles of trail have been opened north of the Catskill Park.

# The Long Path:
# Today and tomorrow

As of 1992, the Long Path is a continuous 236-mile hiking trail which extends from the New Jersey side of the George Washington Bridge to the Town of Ashland on the Greene/Schoharie county line. While plans go ahead to extend the trail to the Mohawk River and the Adirondacks, the existing trail route is constantly changing.

In the late 1970's and in the 1980's, the northward movement of suburbia began to have a major impact on the trail system. Where it was once possible to get permission to build a trail with just a knock on a door and a handshake, formal agreements were now required. The ridgetops where the trails passed were no longer immune to development. In some areas, the trail had to be moved from the woods to public roadways. In other places, bucolic country roads followed by the trail have become suburban thoroughfares.

About 60 miles of the Long Path currently follows public roadways. About 36 miles of this roadwalking is in the Orange County section between Schunemunk Mountain and the Shawangunks. The lack of major geographic features have made it difficult to find suitable off-road locations for the trail in this section, which is prone to development.

In 1989, the New York-New Jersey Trail Conference, in cooperation with the National Park Service, initiated a study to determine the feasibility of relocating the Long Path from the roads of Orange County to the Shawangunk Ridge. The proposed route would follow the Appalachian Trail from Harriman State Park to High Point State Park in the northwest corner of New Jersey and then continue along the Kittatinny-Shawangunk Ridge to

Minnewaska State Park, where it would rejoin the existing Long Path. After two years of study, a report was issued which demonstrated the feasibility of this route, and the Trail Conference began negotiating with local landowners to obtain permission to construct this new trail. As we go to press, agreements have been received from landowners to allow us to construct 30 of the 36 miles of this new trail. It is hoped that major sections of this new trail will be opened during 1992.

While work goes ahead on this Shawangunk Ridge Trail, interest has surfaced from those who wish to preserve the historic route of the Long Path across Orange County. Plans have been developed to relocate the Long Path off the roads by using a series of abandoned railroads and county and state parks. Where these routes are not available, it is proposed to construct a path in the woods parallel to but about ten feet from the roadways. It is hoped that, in the future, the Long Path System will offer two routes from Harriman State Park to Minnewaska State Park—one following a variation of the historic route, and the other utilizing the Appalachian Trail and the newly constructed Shawangunk Ridge route.

In Rockland County, the Long Path passes through a series of state and county parks before entering Harriman State Park. While most of the trail in Rockland County is on public land, there are vital links across private property. Only 30 miles from New York City, this section is the most threatened. Together with the Rockland County Planning Board, the Trail Conference has prepared a report entitled *The Long Path in Rockland County*. This report, which views the Long Path as "the spine of a Rockland County Greenway," is intended to provide guidelines to local planning boards for long-term protection strategies for the trail.

In the Catskill Park, the Long Path follows public roadways in the central Catskill area, primarily around Phoenicia. This roadwalking exists because of a lack of existing trails for the Long Path to follow—not due to the absence of public land. Because the Catskill Forest Preserve is protected by Article 14 of the New York State Constitution—which mandates that it be kept "forever wild"—the construction of new trails is strictly regulated by the New York State Department of Environmental Conservation. Ordinarily, all new trails must be approved as part of the DEC's unit management plan for the area.

The Trail Conference is currently proposing a comprehensive plan for removing the Long Path from roads in the Catskill Park. Part of this plan would involve the construction of a new trail section which would route the Long Path past the proposed Catskill Interpretive Center. This new route would provide a great deal of public visibility for the Long Path and would allow visitors to the Interpretive Center to hike along this trail. It is hoped that the DEC will accept the Trail Conference's plan and that these new trail sections will be constructed in the next few years.

The Trail Conference has also begun a concerted effort to extend the Long Path to the Mohawk River and the Adirondack Park—thus enabling the Long Path to achieve its original goal of a long-distance trail from New York City to the northern Adirondacks. In the last year and a half, the first twelve miles of this new trail section have been built.

In late 1990, the Trail Conference entered into an agreement with the National Park Service to study potential routes for the Long Path from the Catskill Park to the Mohawk River. Three major alternative routes were explored. The selection process included extensive public input, with representatives of the Trail Conference and other organizations exploring each of the three routes. At the end of 1991, the Trail Conference chose its preferred route, which was the historic route laid out by Vincent Schaefer in the 1930's. This route was chosen because it had the most outstanding features of the three routes studied.

The Trail Conference is currently identifying local landowners along the proposed route. Parts of the route already have existing trails, and these will be adopted as part of the Long Path. It is hoped that sections of this new trail will be constructed in 1992. The goal is to have the Catskills-to-Mohawk River section finished by the mid 1990's, and the Long Path completed to the Adirondacks by the year 2000.

**Verkeerder Kill Falls**

# Section 1

*George Washington Bridge to Route 9W at Lamont-Doherty*

| | |
|---|---|
| **Feature** | *Palisades* |

| | |
|---|---|
| **Distance** | *12.7 miles* |

## General description

The Long Path follows the crest of the spectacular Palisades, wandering between the cliff edge and the Palisades Interstate Parkway. The route affords stunning views of the basaltic face of the Palisades, the Hudson River and the City of New York and its suburbs. The trail passes through rich forests, with occasional streams and swamps. Old roads, rock walls and foundations along the route are remnants of past settlement along the Palisades. Several side trails lead down to the Shore Trail along the Hudson River. These allow the hiker to make a number of interesting circuits; the *New York Walk Book* can be consulted for additional information. The trail is generally wide and nearly level (except for some steep sections near the New York-New Jersey border). Unfortunately, the trail is almost always within sound of the Palisades Interstate Parkway.

## Access

*From New York:* Take the George Washington Bridge to the first exit after the Palisades Interstate Parkway.
*From New Jersey:* Take any road—including the Palisades Interstate Parkway, I-95, NJ 4 and US 1-9—that

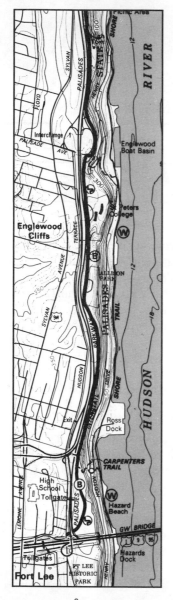

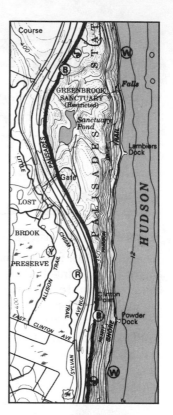

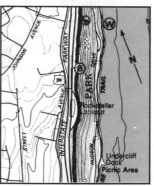

0 ½ 1 Mile

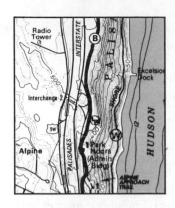

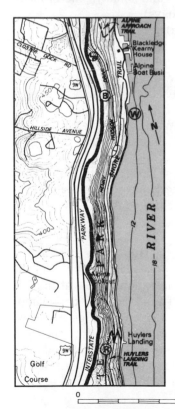

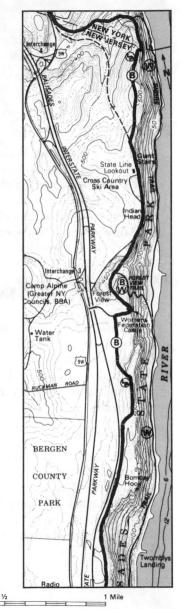

0 ½ 1 Mile

**3**

leads to the George Washington Bridge. The trail begins on Hudson Terrace, which is the easternmost north-south road in the vicinity of the Bridge, just north of the overpass which carries the approach to the Bridge over Hudson Terrace.

## Parking

**0.0** Fort Lee Historic Park, about two blocks south of the trailhead on Hudson Terrace (fee charged April-November); street parking along and near Hudson Terrace (free on Sundays and holidays; meters with one-hour limit on other days).

**1.4** Allison Park (when open).

**3.3** Rockefeller Lookout (20-minute limit).

**6.4** Alpine Lookout (20-minute limit).

**10.4** Parking along Route 9W in Alpine near overpass leading to Women's Federation Castle.

**11.3** State Line Lookout.

**12.7** Parking along Route 9W at state line, just south of the access road to Lamont-Doherty Geological Observatory.

Parking is also available at Ross Dock and the Englewood and Alpine Boat Basins on the Hudson River; side trails lead up to the Long Path (fee charged April-November).

## Trail description

**0.00** The Long Path begins on Hudson Terrace at the steps leading to the northern pedestrian walkway of the George Washington Bridge. Three aqua blazes at the foot of the steps mark the start of the trail. The trail climbs two sets of steps, turns left to cross a bridge roadway, and enters the woods on a broad gravel track to the right of a chain-link fence. Several side paths lead left and right (the Long Path follows the "Trail to River" signs) as the trail affords a few views of the Hudson River.

**0.50** At the last of several signs for "Trail to River," the Carpenters Trail leads, right, to the Shore Trail. The Long Path continues to the left on a narrower track and again runs near the cliff edge. Soon after, a side trail leads left to a footbridge over the Palisades Interstate Parkway, and an old mounted cannon is passed. The trail also goes by several old stone walls and crosses a stream.

**1.15** The trail passes a gas station (*water*, vending machines, *food*, *phone*) on the left. A stream is soon crossed.

**1.40** After passing the park's iron fence on the right, the trail reaches the entrance to Allison Park. This park was developed by the trustees of the Estate of William O. Allison (1849-1924), who was born and spent his life nearby. When open, the park offers *water*, restrooms, *phone*, and overlooks. The Long Path continues along the paved access road to the park, enters a narrow strip of woods near the Parkway, and passes the entrance road to St. Peters College. It then briefly follows the Parkway's shoulder before heading back toward the edge of the Palisades on what soon becomes a cracked asphalt drive.

**2.10** The trail descends steps to Palisade Avenue, turns right, turns left at the corner and goes up steps to the right. It then turns left to follow the cliff edge. Views of the river include the Henry Hudson Bridge and Manhattan's Inwood Hill Park.

**2.75** As the Long Path turns left, an unmarked trail straight ahead leads to the High Tom promontory, with magnificent views up the river.

**3.25** The Long Path reaches Rockefeller Lookout, with its tremendous views. It soon crosses a small stream and briefly follows an old gravel road, with many fine river views. Clinton Point, reached by a short walk from the trail just after an open area is traversed, is one of the best viewpoints. Just after the trail crosses another stream, the fence for the Greenbrook Sanctuary comes in from the right.

**View from High Gutter Point**

**5.10** The trail crosses the entrance road to the Greenbrook Sanctuary. The sanctuary, open to members only, preserves a splendid example of the forests and other habitats that once ranged along the top of the Palisades. The Long Path continues along the sanctuary's fence, twice plunging below the grade of the Parkway to cross over streams that run through woodland swamps.

**5.95** The Huylers Landing Trail (red), which connects with the Shore Trail at the Hudson's edge, leads right at a very sharp angle. The Long Path soon returns to the edge of the Palisades.

**6.45** Alpine Lookout, with many fine views, is reached. The trail runs past the lookout and enters the woods at the end of the cliff-edge railing. The trail passes a series of old stone walls and foundations and travels briefly on an old road as it meanders between the Parkway and the cliff edge. It is never far from either, and views are often possible.

**7.85** A tunnel to the left leads under the Palisades Interstate Parkway to Route 9W.

**8.05** The trail uses a tunnel to pass below Alpine Approach Road. Immediately after the tunnel, the Alpine Approach Trail leads right to the Alpine Boat Basin. The Long Path jogs left at this point and soon comes out of the woods and follows Alpine Approach Road. (For reverse direction, a sign reading "Path to River" shows where the Long Path leaves the paved road and enters the woods).

**8.25** The trail passes the headquarters building of the New Jersey Section of the Palisades Interstate Park. A few hundred yards further, it enters the woods on a wide path at the end of a grassy clearing just beyond the split between the ramps for the northbound and southbound Parkway. The trail now passes through a variety of hardwood and hemlock forests and often affords river views, some quite fine.

**10.00** The trail reaches the end of the old Ruckman Road. To the right is an overlook above the Hudson (with an concrete block wall). The Long Path turns left on Ruckman Road and, in another 50 feet, turns right on a gravel road into well-developed forest. Soon a second gravel road leads right to run along the cliff edge. This road (which is *not* the route of the Long Path) ends in about 900 feet at the end of a great split off the main face of the Palisades. With its many splendid views, it makes a worthwhile side excursion.

**10.40** The trail turns right on a narrow gravel road. In another 500 feet, the Long Path reaches a second gravel road. The left branch, marked with blue-and-white rectangles, leads to a footbridge over the Parkway and to the Bergen Council Boy Scouts' Camp Alpine. To the right, these markers run concurrently with the Long Path.

**10.55** Reach a clearing, with stone castle of the New Jersey State Federation of Women's Clubs. Beyond the clearing, the trail descends on rock steps. A few hundred yards beyond, the blue-and-white trail leaves, right, and descends to the river. The Long Path then crosses a stream and begins to ascend on steps to reach the concrete access road to the State Line Lookout. (This road was originally part of Route 9W). The trail bears right and follows the concrete road past large stones that block vehicle access.

**11.25** The lookout's snack bar, with restrooms, *food*, *water*, and *phone*, is on the left. The concession is open all year. The trail continues along the edge of the concrete road and soon passes Point Lookout (elevation 532 feet), which is the highest point in the New Jersey section of the park. In another 225 yards, the Long Path bears right into the woods just past the end of the rock wall along the roadside.

**11.90** Continue straight ahead as a cross-country ski trail comes in from the left. In another 300 feet, the Long Path turns right, up four steps, and continues on a narrower path. It turns right at a chain-link fence marking the New Jersey-New York state boundary (to the left, there is a stone boundary monument, placed in 1882). The trail descends along the fence on stone steps, turns left, and passes through a gate in the fence. It continues to descend on steps, often quite steeply.

**12.20** The steps end, and the Shore Trail (white) starts to the right. The Long Path descends more gradually to a stream crossing (the bridge has been swept away) and then ascends gently but steadily.

**12.35** An unmarked trail leads right to follow the stream for 0.75 mile to a beautiful cascade to the Hudson. Another unmarked trail leaves to the right 0.2 mile further along the Long Path, as the ascent ends.

**12.70** The Long Path reaches Route 9W at the entrance road to the Lamont-Doherty Geological Observatory, which is just north of the New Jersey-New York state line (end of section). To continue, cross the entrance road and continue along the left side of a chain-link fence.

# Section 2

*Route 9W at Lamont-Doherty to Nyack (Mountainview Avenue)*

| | |
|---|---|
| ***Features*** | *Tallman Mountain State Park, Blauvelt State Park* |

| | |
|---|---|
| ***Distance*** | *9.95 miles* |

## General description

After following the Palisades through New Jersey, the Long Path continues into New York along the Palisades escarpment. This section is a mix of state parks, a county park, a town park, private property, and some suburban road walking. Unlike the true ridgetop route to the south, here the trail takes a roller coaster ride that begins in the valley along Route 9W in Palisades, climbs to Tallman Mountain State Park, descends to the Village of Piermont, ascends again to Mt. Nebo and Blauvelt State Park, and finally descends into Nyack. This section is rich in history, with the trail passing close to historic places such as Sneden's Landing, the Revolutionary village of Palisades, Rockland Cemetery and the abandoned rifle ranges in Blauvelt State Park.

## Access

Take the Palisades Interstate Parkway to Exit 4, which is just south of the New York-New Jersey state line. Turn left (north) onto Route 9W, and follow it to the beginning of the section at the state line, by the entrance to the Lamont-Doherty Geological Observatory.

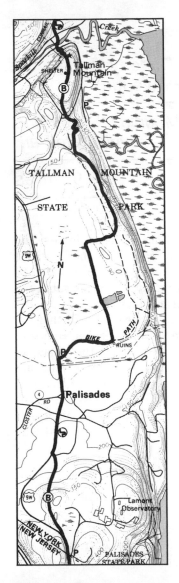

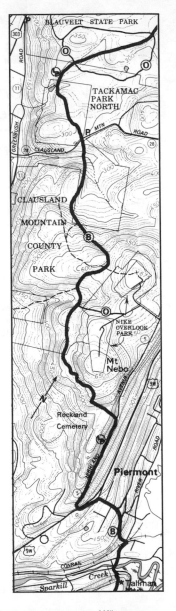

0    ½    1 Mile

## Parking

**0.0** Parking along Route 9W at state line, just south of access road to Lamont-Doherty Geological Observatory.

**1.1** Route 9W at county bike trail.

**2.6** Tallman Mountain State Park.

**3.4** Street parking in Piermont.

**6.5** Takamac Park on Clausland Mountain Road.

**9.9** Street parking in Nyack.

## Trail description

**0.00** The Long Path crosses the entrance to the Lamont-Doherty Geological Observatory and follows to the left of a chainlink fence. It goes through a gate and continues along a woods road. In 200 feet, when the road is blocked by vegetation, turn left and follow a footpath to the north, parallel to Route 9W, and pass a swamp to the right. The trail then crosses a stone wall and ascends over a small knoll.

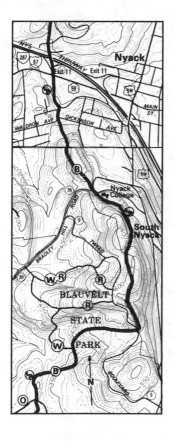

**0.25** Turn right onto a woods road and continue downhill, roughly paralleling Route 9W.

**0.55** The trail reemerges on Route 9W and continues north. In about 0.25 mile, it intersects Washington Spring Road on the right and Oak Tree Road on the left. If you walk right, you will pass through Sneden's Landing. Today, Sneden's Landing is a well-known enclave for artists and actors escaping from the city. Historically, Sneden's Landing was the site of ferry service to Dobbs Ferry in the Revolutionary War. If you walk left, you will pass historic sites such as the DeWitt house in the Village of Tappan, Washington's headquarters in the Revolutionary War. From this intersection, the Long Path continues north along Route 9W.

**1.10** The trail turns right, leaves Route 9W, and enters Tallman Mountain State Park. It passes a parking area and heads east towards the river on a gravel road that is part of a Rockland County bike path and parallelled by a berm. This berm was part of a system built for an oil tank storage facility which was never completed because of strong public opposition.

**1.40** The Long Path turns left off the bike path and follows a woods road through the berm system. The woods road crosses a marshy section on a plank bridge and crosses the bike path. It soon approaches the Palisades escarpment and parallels the river, with good views of the Sparkill Marsh, a golden growth extending out into the river.

**2.60** The trail enters the main picnic area of Tallman Mountain State Park. It continues through the picnic area, goes around the Tallman Park swimming pool, then turns sharply left and ascends on a paved path with a wooden railing to the swimming pool access road. It crosses the road and climbs through the woods on railroad tie steps, gradually at first and then steeply, to the North Hill picnic area.

**2.95** Reaching the North Hill plateau, the trail turns right and follows the North Hill road east and then north along the edge of the escarpment. From here there is an expansive view of the river, from Hook Mountain and the Tappan Zee in the north to the Sparkill Marsh in the south, and almost to the New York-New Jersey state line. The Villages of Irvington and Dobbs Ferry may be seen across the river, with the gothic tower of the Lynd-hurst Mansion imposing on the skyline to the north.

**3.15** The Long Path leaves the escarpment and begins a steep, rocky descent to Sparkill Creek. It soon emerges on a cinder path and finally crosses Sparkill Creek and enters the Village of Piermont. At a flashing yellow light, the trail crosses Paradise Avenue and continues straight ahead on Piermont Avenue.

**3.45** In the center of Piermont, the trail turns left onto Tate Avenue and climbs uphill, then turns right and par-allels the river. Soon the trail turns left and climbs up an old concrete staircase, emerging on Ash Street adjacent to the former Piermont railroad station. (The station building, which is over 100 years old, is now a private residence). The abandoned Erie Railroad right-of-way, which crosses the Long Path here, is now a hiking trail (an official side trail to the Long Path) and provides an interesting alternative path north to Nyack. The trail turns left and continues west along Ash Street, takes the left fork, crosses Route 9W, and continues steeply up Tweed Boulevard (Rockland County Route 5). After an 0.6-mile-long roadwalk, the trail makes a hairpin turn left onto an old woods road, and proceeds up to the crest of the Palisades ridge.

**4.55** The Trail emerges onto Cemetery Road in the Rockland Cemetery. John Charles Fremont (1813-1890), better known as the "Pathfinder," is buried here. The roads in the cemetery pass a number of interesting obe-

**General Fremont's Grave—Rockland Cemetery**

lisks and afford a magnificent view of the Tappan Zee. The Long Path follows Cemetery Road to the right for about 60 yards, then turns right onto a woods road. The trail continues along this road for a short distance, gradually regaining the Palisades ridge. Soon the trail leaves the road and heads north along the western side of the ridge. It then continues on a level path through the woods, crossing several stone walls and intermittent streams.

**5.30** The Long Path arrives at a three-way trail intersection. Here it turns sharply left, then jogs right, starting gradually downhill. At the intersection, an orange-blazed woods road continues straight ahead to Mt. Nebo. Mt. Nebo, which was once a Nike missile site, now is a recreation area for the Town of Orangetown. The Long Path continues downhill, crosses a stream bed, makes a left jog, then goes right, gradually ascending. From here, the trail gradually undulates through the woods, crossing several streams along the way—the last one on a wooden bridge.

**6.50** The trail crosses Clausland Mountain Road and enters Tackamac Park of the Town of Orangetown. The trail passes through a metal gate and descends, first on a gravel road and then on a woods road, until it reaches a small water impoundment. Here the Long Path goes right into the woods, following the water impoundment. Soon the trail crosses the stream and ascends to rejoin the woods road.

**7.00** The trail goes through a gap in a stone wall and enters Blauvelt State Park. A nearby embankment was the site of the firing line for the pre-World War I National Guard Camp Bluefield's rifle range. All the trees in this section were planted after the camp was abandoned by the National Guard because the lead from the bullets kept landing in Grand View, to the east along the river. The Long Path turns right, following the stone wall, and then follows a series of woods roads around the rifle range. The trail soon parallels a target wall of the rifle range.

**7.55** The Long Path climbs over a small embankment and descends a set of wooden steps to a woods road. This embankment is actually the earth-covered concrete tunnel that provided safe passage from the firing line to the target wall. The trail continues to the right along the woods road, passing the entrance to the tunnel on the right. It continues straight ahead, turns sharply left on another woods road, then soon turns right into the woods, at a stream crossing, before finally emerging onto Tweed Boulevard. The Long Path crosses the boulevard and climbs a staircase onto the crest of the Palisades ridge.

**8.50** There is a 180° view here, with the Tappan Zee, Piermont Pier, New York City and the Hackensack River valley all visible. This was the site of the famous "Balanced Rock." Because vandals managed to unbalance it, park officials were forced to remove it in 1966. From here, the trail continues along the ridge before finally descending to a gravel road which leads left to Tweed Boulevard.

**8.90** The trail goes right and soon passes a large blue water tank. It continues on a woods road bordered on the west by a very steep talus slope. Straight ahead, Hook Mountain is visible through the trees. The trail descends behind the Nyack College campus and emerges onto South Highland Avenue, where it passes a number of residences that were once part of the Clarkstown Country Club.

**9.25** The trail turns left on Bradley Boulevard and, after 100 yards, turns right into the woods just before a driveway and regains the Palisades crest.

**9.50** The Long Path passes an opening in an old stone wall, with good views into the Village of Nyack. The trail descends west off the ridge and soon turns right and passes a residential area.

**9.70** The trail emerges onto the end of paved Towt Road. It follows Towt Road, and then turns right onto Waldron Avenue. The apartment complex on the left was formerly a ballfield that was once the home of a minor league baseball team.

**9.95** The trail reaches the intersection of Waldron Avenue and Route 59 (end of section). Here there are a number of motels, stores and fast food restaurants. To continue, proceed straight ahead (the road beyond this point is known as Mountainview Avenue).

# Section 3

*Nyack (Mountainview Avenue) to
Long Clove (Route 9W)*

| | |
|---|---|
| **Feature** | *Hook Mountain* |

| | |
|---|---|
| **Distance** | *8.9 miles* |

### General description

The first two miles of this section are suburban, and the trail frequently runs along roads or near houses. After leaving Route 9W, the Long Path ascends Hook Mountain, whose summit affords splendid views up and down the Hudson River. The trail then continues through gentle woodlands and along ridges.

### Access

Take the New York State Thruway to Exit 11, which is at Mountainview Avenue.

### Parking

**0.0** Strip shopping centers near Mountainview Avenue may provide parking.

**0.2** Street parking on Gail Drive (the first right after the trail crosses the Thruway).

**1.6** Christian Herald Road at Route 9W.

**5.5** Rockland Lake Road (limited, tends to fill up on weekends).

**6.2** Golf course parking lot.

**8.9** Route 9W (limited parking).

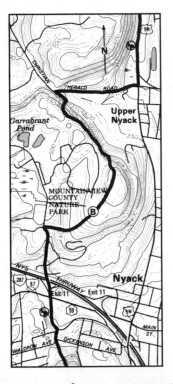

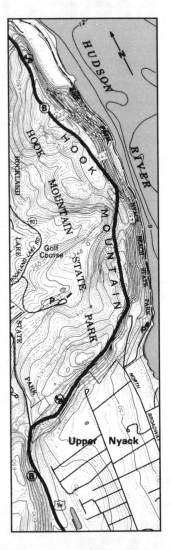

0 ½ 1 Mile

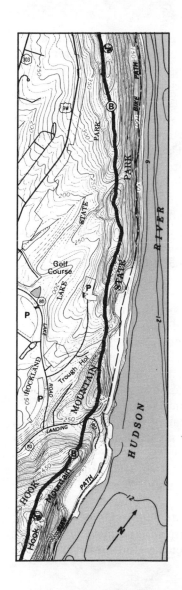

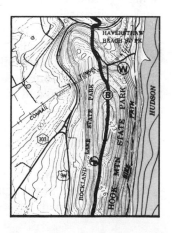

# Trail description

**0.00** The section begins where Waldron Avenue/Mountainview Avenue crosses Route 59. There is a traffic light at the intersection. The Long Path continues north on Mountainview Avenue and heads uphill to the bridge over the New York State Thruway. This is a busy commercial area, with *food* and *phones* widely available. Once the Thruway is crossed, Mountainview Avenue becomes a quiet street and soon passes Gail Drive on the right.

**0.30** The trail turns right onto the first unmarked street after Gail Drive. In 40 feet, it climbs (with no clear footpath) the short embankment on the left side of this street. At the top, the trail enters the woods and climbs gently along a path that parallels Mountainview Avenue. Upon reaching a dirt road, the trail turns right and follows this road as it becomes narrow and grassy.

**0.65** The dirt road ends at the parking lot of a townhouse development. The trail turns right and goes between the parking lot on the left and woods on the right, then turns left at the end of the lot (unmarked) and runs between buildings and woods. Just before the line of buildings makes a diagonal turn to the right, the trail follows a path into the woods that continues to run parallel to the buildings. The trail gradually veers away from the buildings and begins to drop downhill into deciduous forest.

**1.40** At the bottom of a fairly steep slope, the trail reaches a dirt road and makes a left turn. The road soon becomes a footpath.

**1.60** Reach Christian Herald Road and turn right.

**2.00** The Long Path turns left onto Route 9W at a traffic light.

**2.40** The trail turns right into the woods, about 20 feet past a short gap in the guardrail, and moves diagonally away from the road. Views of the Hudson River and the

Tappan Zee Bridge appear, and the trail soon begins the often steep and rocky climb up Hook Mountain.

**3.15** The open, rocky summit of Hook Mountain affords a tremendous view up and down the Hudson River, with the Palisades visible to the south on the right bank of the river. The trail now descends through dry woods. Many fine views occur as the trail trends downward, with occasional uphill stretches, often along a ridge. As the trail approaches the recreation areas of Rockland Lake State Park, an old stone wall is passed and several unmarked side trails leave to either side.

**5.45** After a final steep descent, reach Rockland Lake Road. The Long Path crosses the road and begins to climb. It quickly passes a tiny old cemetery and soon begins to follow up and down the ridge. There are several beautiful views, some from precipices, of Croton Point Park and Croton Dam on the east bank of the Hudson River. The trail passes tennis courts and a stone wall to the left.

**6.25** An unmarked trail leads left to the parking lot of a state park golf course. When open, the concession provides *water*, *phone* and *food*. The Long Path continues along the ridge, often changing from upward to downward, with views through the trees both to the left and to the right.

**8.50** The Long Path makes a sharp left, up a slight grade, as a white-blazed trail continues straight ahead. (This white-blazed trail leads down to the Shore Path). The Long Path crosses under a power line (beneath which there is a railroad tunnel) and descends to Route 9W.

**8.90** The trail reaches Route 9W just east of its intersection with Route 304 (end of section). To continue, cross Route 9W and follow along Long Clove Road.

# Section 4

*Long Clove (Route 9W) to*
*Mt. Ivy (Route 202)*

| | |
|---|---|
| ***Feature*** | *High Tor* |
| ***Distance*** | *6.8 miles* |

### General description

In this section, the Long Path travels along little used
roads for a mile, passing dramatic quarried Palisades
cliffs, then enters woods and ascends High Tor. The ascent is often steep, with several good outlooks. The open
summit affords a 360° view up and down the Hudson Valley. The trail then descends from High Tor, ultimately
passing Little Tor while following the ridge. After crossing Central Highway, the trail enters Rockland County's
South Mountain Park. The section ends by descending off
the western curving edge of the Palisades just before that
feature plunges below the ground.

### Access

This section begins on Route 9W just east of its junction
with Route 304. The trail crosses Route 9W at the sign
for Tilcon New York Inc., in the center of an "S" curve.

### Parking

**0.0** Long Clove Road and Route 9W (limited parking).
**0.2** Tilcon New York headquarters has parking space on
weekends.
**1.0** Along South Mountain Road near Scratchup Road.

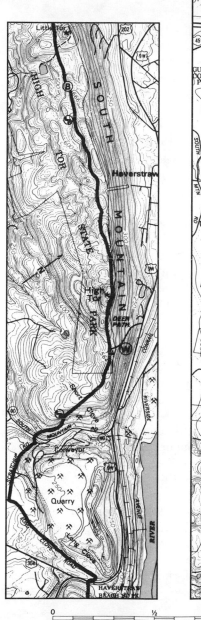

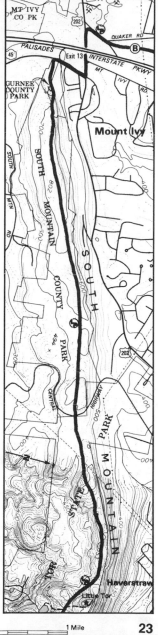

**4.5** Central Highway (limited parking).

**6.8** Mt. Ivy commuter parking lot, open to those with Trail Conference or member club affiliation on non-business days; phone Haverstraw Police at (914) 354-1500 on morning of hike.

## Trail description

**0.00** The section begins at the intersection of Long Clove Road and Route 9W. The trail proceeds northward on Long Clove Road and almost immediately follows the road uphill around a sharp left hook. The name of the street soon changes to Scratchup Road.

**0.60** Follow the road along a sharp right turn. The trail soon passes the gates for the Tilcon New York quarry.

**1.00** The trail swings left and uphill to reach South Mountain Road. It turns right, follows South Mountain Road for about 50 feet, crosses the road and begins the ascent of High Tor by climbing steeply into the woods. The trail soon crosses a pair of stone walls and a power line. The grade then moderates as the trail continues along the top of a broad, gently sloped ridge.

**1.70** In a shallow hollow, the Deer Path, which is blazed white, leaves on the right to descend to Route 9W. The Long Path passes briefly along a cliff edge, with some side trails to a river view. It then turns away from the cliff face to begin the first of four short, extremely steep climbs that often require hand pulls.

**2.10** After the fourth steep rise, reach the summit of High Tor (elevation 832 feet). High Tor is the highest peak on the Palisades, and its open, rocky summit affords spectacular views in all directions. The Hudson River vanishes to the north behind Dunderberg Mountain. Directly below, along the Hudson, is the Town of Haverstraw. Con Edison's Indian Point nuclear plant is visible across from Tomkins Cove. To the west, the peaks of Harriman State Park may be

**Climbing High Tor**

seen. The polygonal pattern visible on the summit's rocks is a natural result of the cooling of the diabase that forms the Palisades. The summit was used by colonists as a signal point during the Revolution, and later was the site of an airplane beacon; the remains of the tower are still visible. The peak was the subject of Maxwell Anderson's play *High Tor*, and conservationists saved it from destruction by trap rock quarrying. The ridge became state property in 1943. The Long Path leaves High Tor and drops steeply into the woods.

**2.25** The trail reaches the end of a fire road that it will follow gently downhill all the way to Central Highway. On the way, it runs through deciduous woods on or near the top of the ridge of the Palisades. The slope is steep to the right and gentle to the left.

**2.85** The Long Path crosses an unmarked trail. To the right, this trail leads to a summit over the cliff edge.

**3.45** Cross an intermittent stream.

**3.50** The trail crosses a dirt road. To the right, the road heads briefly uphill and swings to the front of the open summit of Little Tor. There is a fine view to the north, with Haverstraw directly below. As the Long Path continues gradually descending along the ridge, it is crossed by many side trails and dirt roads.

**4.55** Cross Central Highway and enter Rockland County's South Mountain Park. The trail enters the woods on a gravel road, but almost immediately (just after passing a car barrier) leaves the road and turns right onto a steep path. The trail is generally close to and parallel with the gravel road, and crosses it once.

**5.00** Join the gravel road briefly as it curves left, follow the road for about 50 feet, and leave the road, descending gently to the right. The Long Path is now a wide, well-cleared path through the woods, following the cliff edge of the Palisades.

**6.35** A precipice affords a view of Cheesecote Mountain and Limekiln, Catamount and Horse Stable Mountains. An old quarry and the edge of the Palisades can be seen ahead.

**6.45** A view over an old quarry shows the end of the Palisades. Beyond, the Palisades ridge dips into the ground. The trail follows this last curving ridge downhill.

**6.65** Reach Route 45, cross it and turn right. (For reverse direction, the trail enters the woods just south of a dirt road and a park sign). The trail soon passes the entrance to a commuter parking lot.

**6.80** Reach the intersection of Routes 45 and 202 (end of section). To continue, turn left onto Route 202.

# Section 5

*Mt. Ivy (Route 202) to*
*Lake Skannatati (Seven Lakes Drive)*

| **Feature** | *Harriman State Park* |
|---|---|

| **Distance** | *8.9 miles* |
|---|---|

## General description

The Long Path heads north along the Palisades Inter-state Parkway for about a mile. It then turns west into forest, crosses the South Branch of Minisceongo Creek, and climbs up the side of Cheesecote Mountain before descending past Cheesecote Pond and Letchworth Village Cemetery. The trail briefly follows Calls Hollow Road before turning west into Harriman State Park. Harriman State Park is a stunningly beautiful preserve of lakes, hemlock and hardwood forest, historical trails and sites, wetlands, mountains and ridges. With its proximity to the New York metropolitan area, parts of Harriman may become crowded on weekends and holidays. The hiker may therefore find a weekday or off-season trip more rewarding. On the portion of its route through the Park covered in this section, the Long Path keeps largely to gentle grades until it reaches Lake Skannatati.

## Access

This section begins at the intersection of NY Route 45 and US 202, just east of Exit 13 of the Palisades Inter-state Parkway. The trail turns west off Calls Hollow Road, about 2.6 miles north of Old Route 202 in Ladentown. The section ends at a fisherman's access parking area on Seven Lakes Drive, about 0.75 mile north of Kanawauke Circle.

## Parking

**0.0** Mt. Ivy commuter parking lot, open to those with Trail Conference or member club affiliation on non-business days; phone Haverstraw Police at (914) 354-1500 on morning of hike.

**3.5** Calls Hollow Road (not recommended).

**8.9** Lake Skannatati parking area.

## Camping

**5.5** Big Hill Shelter (0.1 mile from Long Path on white-blazed side trail).

## Trail description

**0.00** At the intersection of Routes 45 and 202, turn west (left) on Route 202. Continue under the Palisades Interstate Parkway.

**0.20** The trail turns right and follows the entrance ramp to the Parkway. After passing Quaker Road to the left, cross the entrance ramp and enter the woods in a small pine grove. For the next 0.7 mile, the trail follows a narrow, forested strip of land between the Palisades Interstate Parkway on the right and a chain-link fence on the left that separates the trail from a housing development.

**0.55** The trail passes under a power line and continues north along the narrow strip.

**1.15** The route becomes very swampy as the chain-link fence veers to the left.

**1.30** The Trail turns right onto a grassy woods road, then turns into the woods and soon begins to parallel the South Branch of Minisceongo Creek.

**1.45** Cross a substantial wooden bridge over the South

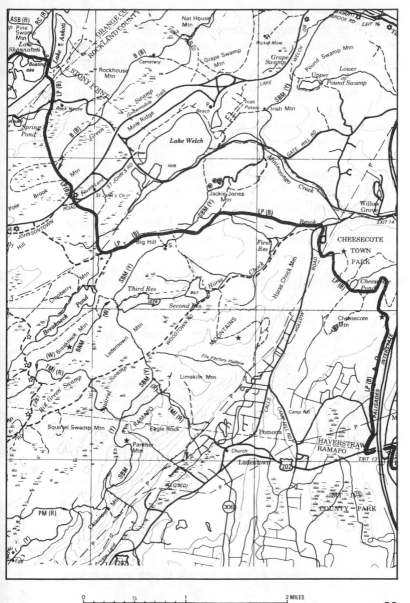

Branch of Minisceongo Creek. The bridge was built in 1984 by participants in the Summer Youth Work Program of Palisades Interstate Park. After crossing the creek, turn right on a woods road. The trail ascends gently through a hardwood forest along a hill slope; a rock wall is on the right.

**1.60** The trail turns left and heads straight up the hill. The grade soon moderates, and the trail continues uphill, with many turns.

**1.90** Turn left on a grassy woods road and continue uphill. The road soon becomes covered with charcoal. From this point, until Calls Hollow Road is reached, many dirt roads diverge from the road that the Long Path follows. However, the trail stays with the largest and most developed road as it twists and turns.

**2.35** Reach the crest of a knob on the shoulder of Cheesecote Mountain and begin to descend, still on the woods road.

**2.45** Reach Cheesecote Pond and turn left. The trail goes along the eastern and southern sides of the pond, with the pond on the right.

**2.60** Reach a large turnaround at the southwest corner of the pond. (Parking at the pond is restricted to Haverstraw residents). The trail bears left and uphill for a short distance, away from the pond. It soon begins a steady descent and changes to a rough cobble base.

**3.30** Shortly after crossing a power line right of way, the trail reaches Letchworth Village Cemetery (where most of the graves are marked only by numbers). It turns left and skirts the cemetery, then turns left again at an intersection of gravel roads. The grade levels off.

**3.50** Reach Calls Hollow Road and turn left along the pavement.

**3.60** Turn right, leaving the road, and re-enter woods. The trail soon crosses Horse Chock Brook on a bridge

**Horse Chock Brook**

built by volunteers of the New York-New Jersey Trail Conference. After crossing the brook, the trail ascends up its valley for a short distance before climbing out and turning left on a woods road, which is frequently cut into the side of the hill slope as it ascends steadily.

**4.15** After a short drop into the valley of an intermittent stream, the Long Path veers right on a narrow track to ascend the valley, while the woods road continues left across the valley. The trail soon crosses the stream and a rock wall as it continues to climb. The forest becomes much more open, with a low understory.

**4.40** Reach a crest, with the hiker's reward for a climb of 500 feet—a large patch of lowbush blueberry. From here it is a short drop and rise to the crest of another small knoll.

**4.55** The trail reaches the dirt road of a buried tele-phone cable right of way. It continues on this road—the route of the Old Turnpike, the original road from South-fields to Haverstraw, built prior to 1824—with gentle ups and downs. (For reverse direction, the trail enters the woods where the right of way makes a hard right turn at post 711).

**5.00** Cross an intermittent stream—a possible source of *water*—that has been running parallel to the left side of the trail.

**5.25** The Suffern-Bear Mountain Trail (yellow) crosses. To the left, this trail leads in 0.35 mile to the Big Hill Shelter.

**5.50** A white-blazed trail leads left 0.1 mile to the Big Hill Shelter. (This short spur is all that remains of the former Skannatati Trail, most of which was absorbed by the Long Path in 1981). The Big Hill Shelter—a substan-tial rock structure—is located on a beautiful site with a fine view. It was rebuilt by the Summer Youth Work Pro-gram in 1988.

**6.10** Reach a narrow paved road (which leads to a camp on Breakneck Pond) and continue straight ahead on it. After about 60 feet, the Long Path turns right, leaving the road, and enters the woods. The trail soon passes through a red pine grove and then descends to a swamp, crossing its outlet on a wooden bridge. The trail goes up and down through a hardwood forest rich in oak. Open forest alternates with patches of dense mountain laurel and occasional boulder fields.

**6.55** The Long Path makes a left turn uphill. Straight ahead, an unmarked trail leads in 0.15 mile to St. John's-in-the-Wilderness Church, the site of the hiking commu-nity's annual Palm Sunday pilgrimage.

**7.05** Turn right and, in 250 feet, cross a grassy road. (In the opposite direction, one must bear right a bit when crossing the road). The trail soon becomes wide and grassy as it approaches Lake Welch Drive.

**7.20** Cross Lake Welch Drive near its intersection with St. John's Road. The Long Path ascends on an old woods road, at first steeply and with several turns, through open, glade-like forest.

**7.40** Bear right, still uphill, as another woods road goes left. In 200 feet, the trail turns left on a narrow path, as the woods road continues straight ahead. After crossing a rock wall, the trail reaches an open knoll with an old stone foundation on the left. Once past the foundation, the trail enters brushier woods and begins to descend.

**7.75** The Beech Trail (blue) starts to the right. A few hundred feet further on, an unmarked trail goes off to the right as the Long Path bears left and begins to descend to an intermittent stream.

**8.30** Cross the rocky outlet stream of a large marsh that is all but hidden to the right. The trail continues on a grassy woods road.

**8.40** Reach Gate Hill Road (also known as Route 106 or Old Route 210), turn right and follow the road for 250 feet. The trail then crosses the road and heads diagonally uphill into the woods. It soon makes a left turn onto a woods road. Two additional left turns bring the trail past the south end of Lake Askoti.

**8.85** Reach Seven Lakes Drive. Turn right, go over the bridge, and enter the woods on the opposite side of the road. The trail descends and swings to the right, passing Lake Skannatati on the left.

**8.90** The trail reaches a paved parking lot (end of section). To continue, follow the shore of Lake Skannatati north through the parking lot.

# Section 6

*Lake Skannatati (Seven Lakes Drive) to
Route 6 (Long Mountain Parkway)*

| **Features** | *Harriman State Park—* |
|---|---|
| | *Surebridge Swamp,* |
| | *Appalachian Trail Crossing,* |
| | *Stockbridge Mountain* |

| **Distance** | *10.15 miles* |
|---|---|

### General description

This section of the trail continues through Harriman
State Park. The Long Path crosses many other trails
within the park, making possible various loop hikes.
The trail traverses hemlock forests and rhododendron
groves, and passes by large swamps. After leaving the
last of the swamps, the trail climbs and follows along the
long, linear ridge of Stockbridge Mountain. Upon descending from the mountain, the trail passes another
swamp before reaching Route 6.

### Access

To reach the beginning of the section from the New York
Thruway, take Exit 15 and continue north on Route 17 to
Sloatsburg. Just north of the village, turn right onto
Seven Lakes Drive. This section starts at the fishing access parking lot off Seven Lakes Drive at Lake Skannatati, about 0.75 mile north of Kanawauke Circle. From
the Palisades Interstate Parkway, take Exit 15, go west

on Gate Hill Road and Route 106 to Kanawauke Circle, then go north for 0.75 mile on Seven Lakes Drive.

## Parking

**0.0** Lake Skannatati parking area.

**5.8** Tiorati Circle picnic area, about 0.5 mile east of the Long Path crossing of Arden Valley Road (fee charged seasonally).

**10.1** Parking area off Route 6.

## Camping

**8.0** Stockbridge Shelter.

## Trail description

**0.00** The section begins at the Lake Skannatati parking area off of the Seven Lakes Drive. Follow the shore of Lake Skannatati north through the parking area. At the northeast end of the lake, turn left into the woods and follow its north shore, as the Arden-Surebridge Trail (A-SB) (red triangle on white) starts to the right. About halfway along the north shore, the Long Path veers away from the lake, crests over a small ridge and drops back to the west arm of the lake. After undulating up and down along the lake's western shore, the trail crosses the lake's swampy inlet stream and begins a series of longer ups and downs.

**1.25** The Long Path turns left and joins a woods road, the route of the Dunning Trail (yellow). After 250 feet, the Long Path turns right on a footpath, as the Dunning Trail continues along the woods road. The Long Path goes over a grassy ledge perched on a hill slope and passes a shaft of the Hogencamp Mine, which was one of the largest iron mines in Harriman Park.

**1.40** The trail turns right near an overhanging rock (known as Cape Horn) to continue up an old stone-lined road. After passing through a saddle, the trail begins to descend through forest rich in hemlock and mountain laurel. It soon joins an old woods road—the continuation of the Surebridge Mine Road.

**2.00** Reach Times Square, the junction of the Long Path, the A-SB Trail (red triangle on white) and the Ramapo-Dunderberg Trail (red dot on white). The Long Path continues west, jointly with the A-SB Trail, on the Surebridge Mine Road, through fairly level terrain.

**2.10** The Long Path and the A-SB Trail turn left, leaving Surebridge Mine Road, and rise gently through a forest of hemlock and white pine. Surebridge Swamp soon becomes visible below to the right. The trail now alternates through laurel, hardwoods, hemlocks and large rhododendrons.

**2.60** The Lichen Trail (blue L on a white square) starts to the left, as the Long Path and A-SB continue on a downgrade to pass a swampy area on the right. The trails approach and veer away from a hemlock swamp and then run along the swamp's intermittent outlet stream before crossing the stream. The descent soon ends as the trails begin to pass a marsh on the right.

**Hikers at Times Square**

**2.90** The White Bar Trail (horizontal white rectangle) starts to the left. In another 30 feet, the Long Path turns right as the A-SB continues straight ahead along the side of a marsh. The Long Path soon crosses an outlet stream and runs between the marsh and a steep, hemlock-covered slope. Upon reaching the head of the marsh, which becomes a wooded swamp, the trail follows an inlet stream. It soon turns left and uphill, away from the stream.

**3.60** Cross the Appalachian Trail (vertical white rectangle) in a slight dip. The trail now rises to a broad knob, dips to a marsh, and climbs a knoll.

**4.30** The trail reaches the top of the knoll and begins to descend, passing a partial view of Upper Lake Cohasset on the way down.

**4.45** Pass a shelter, with no water, on the left, as the descent continues. (This shelter was built in 1937 for the girls' camps on Upper Lake Cohasset). The trail soon crosses Surebridge Mine Road and, in another 0.25 mile, it crosses a stream leading from a marsh on the right to Upper Lake Cohasset. The trail now crosses a series of intermittent streams and boulder fields as it approaches the road.

**5.75** Cross Arden Valley Road at a horseshoe bend. The Long Path jogs left to cross the pavement opposite a wide woods road. Follow this woods road as it passes to the left of a beautiful hardwood swamp.

**6.15** Soon after the swamp ends, the Long Path climbs to the left, as the woods road continues straight ahead. The trail now ascends, sometimes steeply, to the long ridge of Stockbridge Mountain. Once reaching the bedrock outcrop of the ridge, the trail follows the crest northeast, with gentle ups and downs.

**7.80** The trail passes under a large cantilevered rock that juts toward the trail from the west, known as Hippo Rock.

**8.00**  The Stockbridge Shelter is reached after crossing a woods road (the Nawahunta Trail) in a valley. Stockbridge Shelter is a handsome rock-and-mortar structure, with a plank floor. It sits on a rock outcrop, with a fine view to the south. No water is available.

**8.30**  The Long Path drops steeply over a boulder slope. The Cave Shelter is set into an overhang near the base of its rock face. It is damp and hardly an inviting place to spend the night. Again, no water is available. From here, the trend is downhill to Route 6. As the descent progresses, trees get larger and form a closed canopy; blueberry becomes more dominant in the understory.

**9.10**  The trail turns left and passes to the left of a small knob that is the point of a large saddle. After crossing from the right to the left side of a valley and back again, the trail climbs out of the valley. It soon reaches and turns left on a woods road. Upon reaching an embankment above Route 6, the trail turns left and follows above the highway.

**10.00**  At the base of the slope, turn right to drop to the highway. The trail crosses the road and continues up the exit road from the parking area on the north side of Route 6. (This road is the old Route 6, used until 1967, when the present road was opened to traffic).

**10.15**  The section ends shortly after the pavement widens to allow parking. To continue, turn left and enter the woods.

# Section 7

*Route 6 (Long Mountain Parkway) to
Woodbury (Route 32)*

| | |
|---|---|
| ***Features*** | *Harriman State Park—*<br>*Howell, Brooks and*<br>*Blackcap Mountains* |

| | |
|---|---|
| ***Distance*** | *11.0 miles* |

## General description

This section is the last of the three within Harriman
State Park, and is by far the most rugged. The Long
Path climbs three peaks, and the grade is often steep,
both up and down. The exertion is worth the effort because the geology is dramatic, especially in the U-shaped
valley between Howell and Brooks Mountains. The trail
frequently borders the West Point Military Reservation.
The last part of this section is outside of Harriman
State Park and generally follows suburban and rural
roads.

## Access

Take the New York State Thruway to Exit 16, and continue east on Route 6. Or take the Palisades Interstate
Parkway to Exit 18, and continue west on Route 6. The
section starts at a parking area in a narrow, unmarked
loop on the north side of Route 6. Entry by car is one way
from the east side of the loop, about 1.2 miles west of the
Long Mountain Circle.

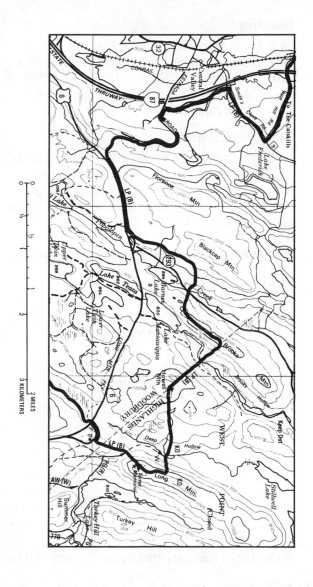

41

## Parking

**0.0** Parking area off Route 6.
**6.1** Barricade on Estrada Road (limited parking).
**11.0** Intersection of Quaker Road and Route 32, about 0.2 mile south of the Long Path's crossing of Route 32 at a railroad trestle.

## Trail description

**0.00** The Long Path leaves the pavement of the parking area loop road and heads north into the woods on a wide gravel road. The road soon becomes grassy as it passes through oak forest with open, short and shrubby understory. The descent into a hollow becomes steeper as traffic noises fade.

**0.30** An old woods road (formerly the route of the Long Path) goes down to the left. Immediately thereafter, the Popolopen Gorge Trail (red square on white) leaves to the right. The Long Path then turns left and begins to climb towards the summit of Long Mountain, following the route of the former Long Mountain Trail. The grade soon steepens.

**0.50** The grade begins to level off as the trail approaches the summit. The vegetation soon becomes sparse.

**0.60** The Long Path reaches the summit of Long Mountain, the site of the Torrey Memorial. Raymond Torrey (1880-1938) served as Chairman of the New York-New Jersey Trail Conference. When Vincent Schaefer of the Mohawk Valley Hiking Club originated the Long Path idea in the 1930's as New York's version of Vermont's Long Trail, Torrey's weekly column in the *New York Post*, "The Long Brown Path," helped popularize the idea and was a highlight to the hiking community. There is a spectacular 360° view from the summit, with Bear Mountain visible to the east, and Turkey Hill Lake directly below.

**Turkey Hill Lake from Long Mountain**

**0.65** The Long Path continues past the Torrey Memorial and begins a gradual descent from Long Mountain. In another 500 feet, the trail turns left and begins a very steep descent through a rocky area.

**1.00** The trail intersects an old woods road (the former route of the Long Path) to the left and crosses Deep Hollow Brook. It then turns right and continues on a path alongside the stream. A second stream soon begins to parallel the trail on the left. Shortly thereafter, the trail turns left at an opening in the woods and crosses the stream on rocks. It then begins to ascend, and soon approaches a cleared swath along the West Point boundary. This boundary line is followed, with some detours to the left, for about half a mile. The trail eventually veers left from the border and tops out at a knoll with lots of blueberry.

**2.05** Reach viewpoint on Howell Mountain, with Brooks Mountain visible to the west, and Blackcap Mountain beyond. Route 6 is visible straight ahead. The trail briefly continues its gentle descent on a curve, slabbing a rise to the right. It abruptly turns left and begins a steep plunge into Brooks Hollow. A flat terrace is quickly traversed before another left turn over the edge completes the descent, this time with switchbacks.

**2.45** Cross the outlet stream from Lake Massawippa in the middle of Brooks Hollow, a classic U-shaped postglacial valley. Its broad, flat floor, with several intermittent stream beds, curves upward on both sides at a rapidly increasing pitch. Once over the log bridge, the trail turns left and goes upstream for a short distance before continuing across the valley floor. Soon the valley wall is reached, and the trail begins a steep ascent of Brooks Mountain, principally by two long switchbacks. The second switchback becomes more gentle in grade as it merges with the southwest trending crest of Brooks Mountain. Once on the crest, the grade is gently uphill, with views of the steeply plunging valley to the left.

**3.10** The ridge ends suddenly at a rocky knob. The Long Path descends steeply to the left and curves to the right, around the end of the ridge. It soon reaches and climbs out

**Stream in Brooks Hollow**

of a small valley, with Lake Massawippa a few hundred feet downhill to the left. The trail undulates up and down as laurel replaces blueberry as the dominant understory plant.

**3.60** Reach Route 293 near a stream. Cross the road at the end of the guardrail and re-enter the woods. The trail now ascends, often steeply, up the shoulder of Blackcap Mountain. Once attained, the ridge crest is followed southwest, closely paralleling the West Point boundary, until the trail descends towards Route 6.

**4.95** The trail approaches Route 6 and turns right (west) along the highway. The blazes are about 30 feet inside the woods bordering the road, next to the chain-link fence. (In the reverse direction, the trail enters the woods about 30 feet west of the "Yield" sign for Route 293 traffic entering Route 6).

**5.50** Just before a large grassy clearing with a power line on the north side of the highway, the trail passes through a gap in the chain-link fence that has been bordering the highway. It veers to the right and crosses the clearing on a diagonal to the northwest. At the opposite side of the clearing, there is a telephone pole at the end of an abandoned paved road (the old Route 6). Turn right and follow this road.

**6.10** Reach a barricade across the road, with a small parking area is on the opposite side. The trail continues straight ahead on what is now known as Estrada Road, a quiet residential street, past several houses. Thomas Estrada-Palma, the first President of Cuba (1902-1906), lived here from 1879 to 1902 while he headed a junta which financed the Cuban Revolution.

**6.55** The trail continues straight ahead as the road becomes paved where several driveways leave it.

**7.05** Continue, still straight, on Estrada Road. In 200 feet, in sight of the New York Thruway, turn right onto Falkirk Road. The trail now follows quiet rural roads.

**7.85** At a T-intersection, go right on Smith Clove Road (Orange County Route 9) and head away from the Thruway.

**8.35** Pass golf course entrance on right.

**8.45** Go left on Pine Hill Road.

**8.70** Pass Pearce Road on the right.

**8.85** Pass Pine Hill Court on the right.

**8.95** Pass De Santis Drive on the left.

**9.05** Pass Skyline Drive on the right. Cross the Thruway and follow Pine Hill Road downhill as it curves.

**9.25** Pass Pine Place on the right.

**9.35** Follow Pine Hill Road under the railroad.

**9.45** Just before Pine Hill Road crosses Woodbury Creek, the Long Path turns right on a gravel road which runs between the railroad tracks and Woodbury Creek.

**10.35** Cross a seasonal stream.

**10.95** Cross Woodbury Creek. This stream crossing may be difficult during periods of high water. If it can't be crossed at the pipeline, follow the shore downstream under the trestle to the road. *DO NOT CROSS THE TRESTLE!* (This railroad trestle, part of what was formerly known as the Graham Line of the Erie Railroad, is now used by Metro-North for passenger service).

**11.00** Reach Route 32. Turn right and go under the trestle. The section ends about 50 feet north of the trestle, where the Long Path turns left and climbs an embankment.

# Section 8

*Woodbury (Route 32) to*
*Salisbury Mills (Route 94)*

| **Feature** | *Schunemunk Mountain* |
| --- | --- |

| **Distance** | *9.1 miles* |
| --- | --- |

## General description

The trail continues for a short distance along a railroad right-of-way before turning into the woods. It soon begins the often steep ascent of Schunemunk Mountain. Schunemunk (pronounced "skun-uh-munk") is a northeast-southwest trending ridge, with sharp sides and a nearly level top. The north half of the mountain is divided by a cleft into two ridges. The Long Path follows much of the length of the western ridge, often with splendid scenery, before it descends to the valley to the west, emerging onto Clove Road at the Hil-Mar complex. The trail follows Clove Road north and goes west along an abandoned road north of Woodcock Hill. The trail then turns north, crosses Woodcock Mountain Road, and follows an abandoned railroad right-of-way across Moodna Creek. It continues along the creek until the section ends at Route 94 in Salisbury Mills.

## Access

Take the New York State Thruway north to Exit 16. Continue north on Route 32 (which is a continuation to the north of Route 17). Approximately 1.8 miles north of the Woodbury Police sign in the town of Highland Mills, you will pass under a high railroad trestle. The Long Path leaves the west side of the road about 50 feet north of the trestle.

## Parking

**0.0** At the intersection of Quaker Road and Route 32, about 0.2 mile south of the railroad trestle.

**6.9** Parking available at the Hil-Mar complex off of Clove Road. Hikers should park in a grassy area just past a garage; do not park in the paved parking lot.

**9.1** Limited parking in Salisbury Mills, just east of Station Road.

## Trail description

**0.00** The Long Path leaves the west side of Route 32 at the end of the guardrail about 50 feet north of where the high railroad trestle goes over the road. It almost immediately climbs a wooded embankment, crosses under the trestle on a gravel road, climbs a steep embankment (watch for poison ivy), and turns right to follow along the left side of the trestle. It soon reaches the grade of the tracks and follows them north.

**0.25** Turn left on a dirt track through a narrow clearing. The trail soon veers right onto a gravel road and heads uphill. Three hundred yards further on, the trail veers right, into the woods (marked with a big rock, well hidden in the vegetation), as the gravel road curls to the left. It crosses a streambed and then a rock wall as it heads uphill. Watch the trail markings very carefully at this point. After crossing a second rock wall, the Long Path makes a sharp right onto the remnants of a woods road.

**0.85** The trail turns left onto a narrow track and heads straight uphill. It now ascends steadily, sometimes steeply up the slope and sometimes more gently across

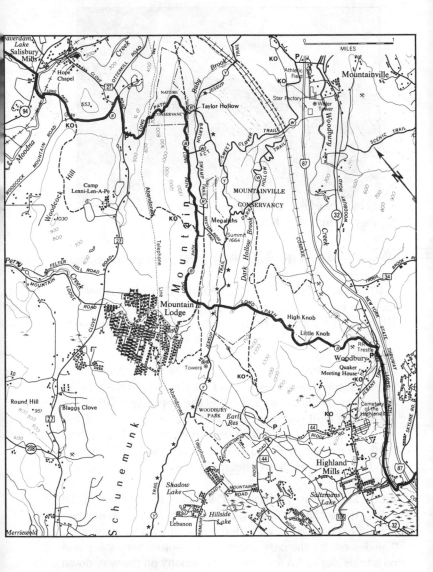

**View from Little Knob**

the slope. Along the way are several good views, including one at Little Knob.

**1.40** Reach the crest of High Knob. This open ridge top has fine views up and down the valley and of the Hudson River to the north. The trail descends off the ridge and soon goes left on rocks forming the west side of the ridge. As it descends, it approaches the head of the valley between High Knob and the ridge to the west. As the gap between the ridges closes, the trail drops into the woods, crosses two valleys, and ascends the opposite ridge.

**1.80** The trail reaches the top of the ridge, which it follows for about 0.4 mile. The trail then drops into a valley.

**2.40** The trail crosses Dark Hollow Brook, which may be dry, and climbs to the main ridge of Schunemunk Mountain.

**2.60** The Jessup Trail (yellow) crosses near the top of the ridge. In another 300 yards, the Long Path reaches an open area of exposed rock, turns left and soon enters the woods. The descent for the next quarter mile is often very steep and on a talus slope. An opening in the canopy on the way down affords views of the lowlands below Schunemunk. Once the base of the talus slope is reached, the descent moderates. Striped maple, a small tree with beautiful variegated bark, is abundant here and well worth watching for.

**2.95** Cross a woods road on level ground. The trail crosses a sometimes swampy intermittent stream, turns left on the next woods road, and soon takes a right fork up a small hill. Less than 50 yards beyond the fork, a narrow track leads diagonally off the woods road to the right (pay careful attention to blazes here). The trail now goes gently uphill through sparse woods, with lots of chestnut oak, and soon gains the westernmost ridge of Schunemunk Mountain. It continues to ascend gently, with occasional views both east and west.

**4.10** The Barton Swamp Trail (red dot on white), which follows a valley between the eastern and western ridges of Schunemunk Mountain, leaves to the right. The Long Path continues straight ahead. (The former route of the Long Path, which turned left at this point to descend off the ridge, is closed to hikers).

**Little Knob and High Knob**

**4.20** The Western Ridge Trail (blue dot on white) leaves to the right. (Until 1992, the Western Ridge Trail also continued north along the western ridge of Schunemunk, following what is now the route of the Long Path). For the next 1.4 miles, the Long Path takes advantage of the many fine viewpoints and interesting rock formations along the way, leading to frequent zig-zags. The trail is marked by both blazes and cairns. Scattered over the windswept top of Schunemunk are pitch pine, birch, oak, elm and many other stunted trees. Blueberry bushes abound, and mountain laurel is found along the lower portions of the trail. Hikers should note that while most of the mountain is closed to hunters, the western areas of the mountain are open for hunting. Hikers should be aware of the dates of the various hunting seasons and plan accordingly. Deer and turkey are often seen on Schunemunk. The geology of this area is quite unique and interesting. The pink conglomerate rock that is found on top of Schunemunk is very different from the rocks found in the other surrounding mountain ranges: the Palisades, the Hudson Highlands, the Ramapos, the Shawangunks and the Catskills.

**4.90** Reach an open area on top of the ridge, with fine views to the west toward Woodcock Hill and beyond to Washingtonville (and on clear days all the way to the ridge of the Shawangunks) and, to the east, of the steep cliffs of the eastern ridge of Schunemunk.

**5.10** The Sweet Clover Trail (white), which crosses to the eastern ridge and continues down to Mountainville, leaves to the right.

**5.60** The Long Path turns left, as the Barton Swamp Trail (red dot on white) continues straight ahead along the ridge. After traversing some more rock outcroppings, the Long Path begins a gradual descent down the western slope of the mountain.

**5.90** The descent becomes steeper as the trail begins to

follow a stream bed (which may be flooded in the spring and immediately following heavy rains).

**6.00** The trail widens and becomes an abandoned woods road, cut into the slope of the mountain and built up with rocks on the downhill side. The road descends gradually on switchbacks.

**6.50** As the road curves to the right, just before a stone wall, the Long Path continues straight ahead, leaving the road, and passes through a gap in the stone wall. The trail continues through some woods for about 75 yards and then turns left onto another woods road. There are several muddy stretches along this road.

**6.70** The trail crosses over a stream and bears to the right, still following the woods road.

**6.90** A private dwelling becomes visible. The trail continues down a paved driveway to the Hil-Mar complex (a small summer vacation retreat with apartments, a pool, and other recreational facilities). The owner allows hikers to park on the grassy area just beyond the garage. Do not park in the paved parking lot.

**Schunemunk Mountain and the Moodna Viaduct**

**7.00** Turn right onto Clove Road. Continue north along the road for 0.5 mile.

**7.50** The trail turns left onto an abandoned paved road, which is currently a private driveway. The condition of the pavement soon worsens as the trail continues along the road, gradually ascending. The road goes mainly through woods, but also passes several fields and a small pond used for ice hockey in the winter.

**7.90** The road begins to descend.

**8.10** The trail turns right, leaving the road, and enters an open field. Follow along the right side of the field. The trail re-enters the woods at the far end of the field. The trees here are very thin, and the blazes may be difficult to see. The trail meanders a bit, crossing stone walls in several places, and follows stream beds which may frequently be muddy.

**8.40** Cross a rutted woods road.

**8.60** Reach paved Woodcock Mountain Road. The Long Path crosses the road and goes into the yard of a private home. Keep to the far right of the yard and follow close to a stone wall.

**8.70** The trail turns left onto an abandoned railbed (which often sees use by motorized vehicles, since it continues for several miles in either direction).

**8.80** Arrive at railroad bridge across Moodna Creek. The bridge is currently in very poor condition, so extreme caution must be used in crossing the creek. After crossing the bridge, the trail turns right, leaving the railbed, and follows along the creek. The route may be muddy in places and it is possible to cut across properties to the left—especially by Weir's Ice Cream Stand—and reach Route 94, then turn right and follow Route 94 to Station Road.

**9.10** The trail crosses Route 94 at Station Road in Salisbury Mills (end of section). To continue, proceed north on Station Road.

# Section 9

*Salisbury Mills (Route 94) to*
*Rock Tavern (Route 207)*

---

**Feature**    *New York, Ontario & Western*
                           *Railroad right-of-way*

---

**Distance**                              *7.0 miles*

---

### General description

After following paved Station Road for 2.6 miles, the
Long Path continues along the right-of-way of the long-
abandoned New York, Ontario & Western Railroad. The
NYO&W once was the primary route to the southern
Catskills, and was responsible for opening up this area to
the masses in the 1800's. However, it was one of the earliest railroads to fall upon hard times, and was abandoned
in the 1950's. The trail in this section is probably one of
America's first rail-to-trail conversions. However, the
right-of-way has reverted to private landowners, some of
whom have given the Trail Conference permission to
route the Long Path over their property. For the most
part, the trail follows the railbed, but in some places it
has been relocated to the sides of the right-of-way, due to
drainage problems in the railbed.

### Access

Take the New York State Thruway to Exit 16 in Harriman. Go west on Route 17 (the Quickway) to Exit 130.
Follow Route 208 north to Clove Road. Turn right
on Clove Road (County Route 27) and continue to Salis-

bury Mills. Turn left and go to Route 94 and Station Road.

## Parking

**0.0** Limited parking in Salisbury Mills, just east of Station Road.

**7.0** Route 207 at Rock Tavern.

## Trail description

**0.00** From Route 94 in Salisbury Mills, the Long Path goes north on Station Road and passes through a residential area.

**2.10** Cross under railroad tracks. This line was formerly known as the Graham Line of the Erie Railroad, and was used for freight trains only, but it is now the route of Metro-North commuter trains to Port Jervis that formerly followed the Erie Railroad main line through Monroe, Goshen and Middletown (now abandoned and being converted into a rail-trail from Harriman to Middletown). You can get to this section on public transportation by taking a train from Hoboken to the nearby Salisbury Mills station.

**2.60** Just before a short hill, bear left on an old unpaved road. Pass the foundation of a station that gave Station Road its name and turn left on the former railbed of the New York, Ontario & Western Railroad. The right-of-way soon becomes wide and open as it passes a housing development on the left. Soon the trail leaves the railbed and follows the embankment to the left to avoid a swampy area. It then crosses over to an embankment on the right and emerges on Toleman Road.

**3.20** Cross Toleman Road and continue on the embankment to the right of the railbed. The trail soon descends to the railbed and continues to Bull Road.

**3.40** Arrive at Bull Road. Here, access to the NYO&W right-of-way is currently restricted by the landowner, so

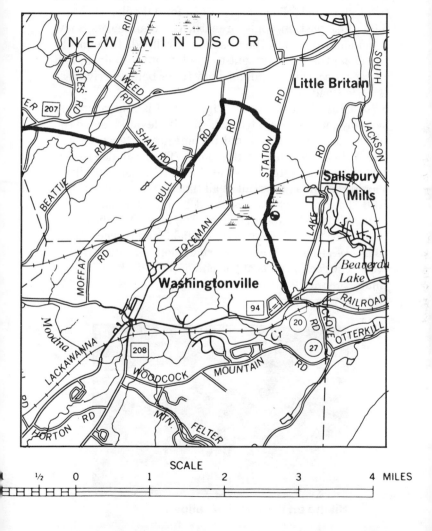

SCALE

½   0        1         2         3         4  MILES

the Long Path turns left onto Bull Road, which it follows for 1.0 mile.

**4.40** Arrive at the intersection of Shaw Road. The trail turns right and follows Shaw Road for 0.6 mile.

**5.00** Just past an apple orchard, the trail leaves Shaw Road and returns to the abandoned railbed. It begins to run along the embankment to the left of the railbed, and crosses the swampy railbed a few times before arriving at Beattie Road.

**5.70** Cross Beattie Road. The railbed is still relatively swampy for 0.1 mile, after which it is elevated above the surrounding marshland and becomes a dry gravel road. You will pass a house at this point. The road also serves serves as a private driveway for this house, so hikers should remain on the trail at all times.

**6.80** The driveway reaches paved Twin Arch Road. Continue on this road for about 500 feet. The Long Path then turns right, goes through an overgrown field, and reaches Route 207. Cross Route 207 and turn right along the guardrail.

**7.00** The section ends at the end of the guardrail. To continue, turn left and proceed along the former NYO&W right-of-way.

**Hiking on the NYO&W railbed**

# Section 10

*Rock Tavern (Route 207) to
Montgomery (Route 17K)*

| | |
|---|---|
| **Feature** | *Mostly Road Walking* |

| | |
|---|---|
| **Distance** | *7.6 miles* |

### General description

The Long Path continues along the abandoned New York,
Ontario & Western Railroad right-of-way for the first 1.4
miles. Initially in a deep cut, it emerges along a power
line before leaving the railbed. From here, the trail follows roads which soon pass through the southwest corner
of the Stewart Airport buffer zone. At the end of the
Stewart property, the trail passes through the former
rail yards of the New Haven Railroad. It then goes
through Maybrook and follows roads to Montgomery.

### Access

Take the New York State Thruway to Exit 16 in Harri-
man. Go west on Route 17 (the Quickway) to Exit 130.
Follow Route 208 north to Route 207. Turn right (east) on
Route 207, and follow it to Twin Arch Road and Forrester
Road in Rock Tavern.

### Parking

**0.0** Route 207 at Rock Tavern.
**7.4** Veteran's Memorial Park in Montgomery.
Parking is also available at many other locations along the
roadwalking section.

## Trail description

**0.00** Descend from Route 207 at the east end of the guardrail. The trail continues to follow the right-of-way of the former New York, Ontario & Western Railroad, but soon leaves the railbed and continues along the embankment.

**0.40** Pass under the skeleton of an old iron bridge (keep off).

**0.60** Reach clearing for power-line access. Bear left and follow the power lines. The power lines are the high voltage lines of the Marcy South system, which carry power from Canada to the northeastern United States.

**1.00** Descend to cross Route 208, then cross a fence and continue on the power line right-of-way (former railbed).

**1.40** Reach Station Road. From here the NYO&W Railroad headed west, passing through the Wurtsboro Tunnel and continuing through the southern Catskills. Much of the right-of-way west of here is no longer visible. The Long Path turns right, leaving the railbed, and continues north on Station Road, passing farms.

**1.90** Turn left onto Route 208.

**2.00** Turn right onto abandoned Barron Road and enter the buffer zone for Stewart Airport, a wildlife preserve. Hunting is allowed here during season, so be sure to follow the marked trail. When the road forks after a few hundred yards, bear left, continuing on semi-paved Decker Road.

**2.60** Arrive at the former rail yard of the New Haven Railroad. This was the westernmost outpost of the New Haven Railroad, located a short distance from its interchange with other lines. Maybrook was once an important railroad junction. The yards were used until the 1970's, when the Poughkeepsie rail bridge was burned, eliminating rail access to the east. Continue straight

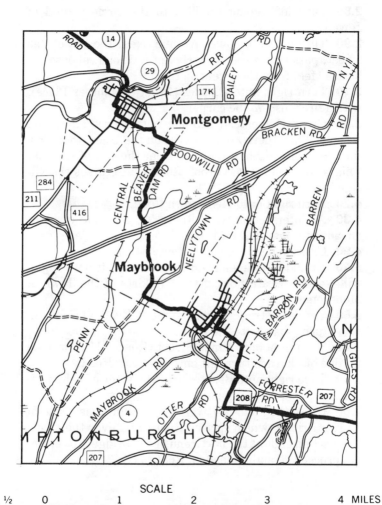

SCALE

1    ½    0    1    2    3    4 MILES

across tracks and turn right (look for blazes on concrete loading platform).

**2.80** Turn left, going uphill onto the circle at end of Jewell Street.

**2.90** Turn left onto Tower Avenue. Near the end of this street, pass an old red New Haven Railroad caboose set back 50 feet from the street on the left.

**3.10** Turn right onto Charles Street (Volunteer Place), with a firehouse on the corner.

**3.20** Cross Homestead Avenue onto Clark Place and ascend. When there are no leaves on the trees, there is a fine view of the Shawangunks from the top of the hill. This road becomes Maybrook Road as it crosses the village boundary.

**4.20** Turn right onto Neelytown Road.

**4.30** At intersection with Route 99, continue straight ahead onto Beaver Dam Road.

**4.90** Cross under Interstate Route 84.

**6.40** At end of Beaver Dam Road, turn left onto Goodwill Road. You are now in the outskirts of the Town of Montgomery.

**6.60** Continue straight ahead on Boyd Road, as Goodwill Road turns sharply to the right.

**7.20** Turn right onto Union Street (Route 211), continue for one block, then turn left onto Bachelor Road.

**7.40** Turn right onto Bridge Street at Veteran's Memorial Park (picnic tables, toilets).

**7.60** Cross the Wallkill River on the right (east) side of Ward's Bridge, which carries Route 17K over the river. The section ends at the north end of the bridge. To continue, proceed straight ahead on Route 17K.

# Section 11

*Montgomery (Route 17K) to
Ulsterville (Route 52)*

| | |
|---|---|
| ***Feature*** | *Road Walking* |

| | |
|---|---|
| ***Distance*** | *11.2 miles* |

## General description

From Montgomery, the Long Path follows roads as it approaches the Shawangunks. The roads in this section were once all back roads and country roads, but spreading development has resulted in the area assuming more of a suburban character. However, there are still sections of forests and farms, with many views of the Shawangunk Mountains in the distance. The section ends at Route 52, a few miles from the Long Path's entrance into the Shawangunks.

## Access

Take the New York State Thruway to Exit 17 in Newburgh. Continue west on Interstate Route 84 to Exit 5. Follow Route 208 north to Route 17K. Turn left (north) on Route 17K and follow into the center of Montgomery. The section begins at the north edge of the bridge over the Wallkill River.

## Parking

**0.0** Route 17K in Montgomery.
**11.2** Route 52 in Ulsterville.
Parking is also available at many other locations along this roadwalking section.

## Trail description

**0.00** From the north end of the Route 17K bridge over the Wallkill River, continue along Route 17K. Stay on Route 17K past Montgomery Road. At this intersection, there is a seasonal farm stand selling vegetables and fruits.

**0.30** Turn right onto Corbett Road. As this road ascends the hill, it changes direction several times.

**2.40** Turn right onto Winding Hills Road (formerly Valley Road).

**2.70** Continue on Winding Hills Road as it makes a sharp left turn (Judson Road goes straight ahead).

**4.10** Turn right onto Youngblood Road.

**4.80** Turn right onto Collabar Road.

**5.30** In Searsville, turn right onto Bullville Road (County Route 43).

**5.50** Opposite a small store, turn left onto County Route 17.

**5.80** Turn right onto Howell Street.

**6.60** Continue straight onto Warn Avenue, as Howell Street turns right.

**7.50** Jog across Route 302 onto Bruyn Avenue. This road has been designated a State Scenic Highway. There is a magnificent view of the entire Shawangunk ridge at this point—the first opportunity for the hiker to see the panorama of the entire ridge.

**8.40** Cross Gillespie Street.

**9.40** Turn right onto Crawford Road, which crosses the Shawangunk Kill. At the other side of the bridge, the road enters Ulster County and its name changes to Shawangunk Lake Road.

**9.70** Turn right onto County Route 7.

**10:10** Turn left onto Lake Shore Drive, passing through a community of small cottages. (Swimming in the lake is prohibited).

**11.20** Reach Route 52 in Ulsterville (end of section). To continue, turn right onto Route 52.

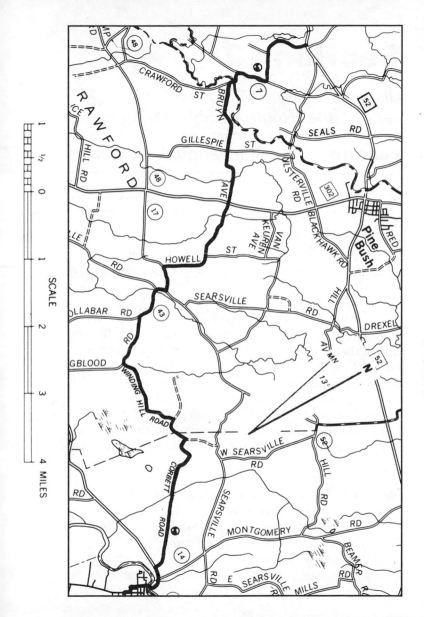

65

# Section 12

*Ulsterville (Route 52) to*
*Jenny Lane (Route 44/55)*

| | |
|---|---|
| **Feature** | *Shawangunk Mountains* |

| | |
|---|---|
| **Distance** | *16.8 miles* |

### General description

After about five miles on quiet country roads, the Long Path enters the woods and begins to climb the Shawangunk Mountains. The Shawangunks are one of New York's most spectacular scenic features. Capped by a hard, white conglomerate, the Shawangunks form a long mountain ridge with gently dipping slopes along the surface of the conglomerate that give way suddenly to great white cliffs. A favored spot for rock climbers, the cliffs provide wonderful views of forested and farmed land in the valley below. The trail is quite rugged where sections of the cliffs are traversed. The trail passes by two lakes, Mud Pond and Lake Awosting. Lake Awosting especially is a gem, with wooded shores that plunge into clear, deep blue water.

**Note:** *The Long Path is currently closed from Upper Mountain Road to Verkeerder Kill Falls. Please do not use the old trail route. As we go to press, the Palisades Interstate Park Commission is arranging for the purchase of land to allow access from Upper Mountain Road to the falls. For further information, please write the New York-New Jersey Trail Conference at 232 Madison*

*Avenue, Room 908, New York, New York 10016, or call (212) 685-9699.*

## Access

Take the New York State Thruway to Exit 17 in Newburgh. Continue west on Interstate Route 84 to Exit 5. Follow Route 208 north to Route 52. Turn left onto Route 52 and follow it west to Ulsterville.

## Parking

**0.0** Route 52 in Ulsterville.

**16.6** Minnewaska State Park parking area on Route 44/55, about 0.75 mile south of the trail crossing.

**16.8** Parking area at Jenny Lane.

## Trail description

**0.00** From the intersection of Lake Shore Drive and Route 52, proceed south on Route 52.

**0.05** The trail turns left onto Quannacut Road.

**0.80** Pass through a stone gate on Quannacut Road. Soon the trail passes the Willow Tree Resort.

**1.05** The trail passes a dam and Murrays Pond on the left. Continue on Quannacut Road, which soon enters a new subdivision.

**1.95** Quannacut Road ends. The trail enters the woods and crosses a Forest Preserve parcel. The trail through the woods is flat.

**2.15** The trail leaves the Forest Preserve parcel and crosses into private property.

**2.25** The trail emerges on a woods road, which soon enters a recently logged area. The road widens and there is evidence of future construction here. Soon the trail passes several Norway spruce trees.

**2.65** Turn right onto Registro Road at a power line

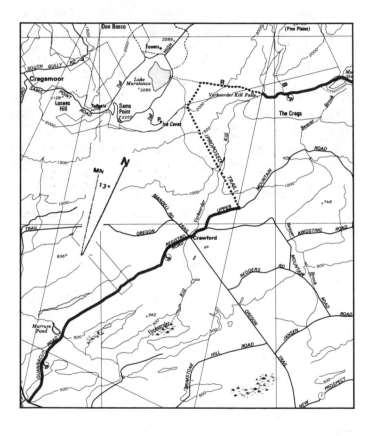

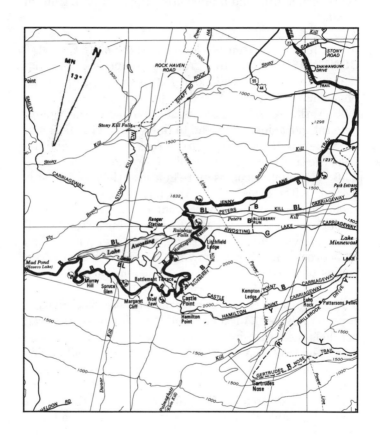

crossing (paving begins here). Follow the narrow paved road past houses.

**2.95** Turn right at Oregon Trail, cross bridge over the Veerkeerder Kill, and immediately turn left onto Church Road.

**3.25** A paved road (Upper Mountain Road) goes off to the left. [The trail is closed at this point. **DO NOT CONTINUE!** Contact the Trail Conference for information on the route of the Long Path from here up to the Shawangunk Ridge].

**6.05** Verkeerder Kill Falls is at the head of the valley. Several short side trails lead to fine views of the falls and the valley, with good exposure of rock strata. Beyond the falls, the trail soon begins to climb through shrub forest.

**6.30** The climb becomes more gentle as the ridge crest is gained. After a lookout to the left on a conglomerate shelf, the trail veers away from the edge and passes through an area covered with blueberry bushes and small trees. Now on fairly level to descending ground—often on bedrock with cairns showing the way—the trail soon begins to follow along a crest, as it approaches a large ridge that enters from the right.

**6.95** Make a sharp left at a cairn, and soon pass above a swamp to the left. Views of Mud Pond appear as the trail parallels the north shore.

**7.35** The trail drops to the level of the pond and begins to run through swampy ground, sometimes on board-walks.

**7.45** Cross the outlet of Mud Pond and continue on a nearly flat table through blueberry, with scattered pine and birch.

**8.35** After a short descent, reach a carriage road near the west end of Lake Awosting. Turn right and follow the road along the shore of the lake. In 200 feet, the trail turns right, off the lakeshore road, onto another carriage

**Hikers at Lake Awosting**

road. (Further down the shore is a swimming beach that may be used when a lifeguard is present. Continuing along the shore will cut some distance and time off the hiker's route, but at the expense of wonderful scenery). The Long Path now ascends gently through scrubby pine forest, following the route of the former—and exceptionally well named—Scenic Trail. Some faded yellow blazes may still be visible.

**8.75** Reach the edge of the ridge, with views to the south and west. The ledges are vertical faces of white, bedded conglomerate. The carriage road twists uphill to reach a higher outlook ledge on Murray Hill, with a 270° view that includes the Hudson Valley to the southeast and the great ridge of the Shawangunks to the northeast. The carriage road ends here, and the Long Path follows a footpath along the ledge. The route—which is often bare and marked by cairns—is nearly flat, with occasional sharp, short climbs or drops. The vegetation is generally short and scrubby.

**9.00** Attain a high point with a 360° view that includes

Lake Awosting. After a short drop, the trail goes left on the overgrown remnants of a carriage road for about 125 feet, and then turns right onto a footpath.

**9.40** The Long Path turns right, onto another carriage road. In 250 feet, it turns left and uphill on a path, soon reaching a decayed carriage road.

**9.65** Soon after the carriage road ends, the trail emerges onto Margaret Cliff, with good views. The trail continues to run along the edge of the cliff.

**10.15** The trail drops steeply, at first through a cleft in the rock, until reaching the base of the rock cliff. It soon moves away from the cliff, crosses a carriage road and then a stream, and ascends through the woods.

**10.35** The trail goes through a natural tunnel in the rock, which is dark, narrow and damp. (Hikers, especially those with packs, can detour around the tunnel by going about 15 feet to the right). The trail emerges in a cleft between rocks and passes below an overhanging rock. It soon reaches a cliff top, with several views.

**10.80** Turn right onto the Hamilton Point Carriage-

**Emerging from the tunnel**

**Castle Point**

way. In 20 feet, the Castle Point Carriageway leaves to the left, as the Long Path continues straight ahead on the Hamilton Point Carriageway. (For reverse direction, continue straight ahead on the Hamilton Point Carriageway, as the Castle Point Carriageway leaves to the right).

**10.90** Turn left off the carriageway onto a footpath and climb. The ascent soon becomes very steep and requires hand pulls up ledges. Very good views appear.

**11.00** Reach Castle Point and turn left onto the Castle Point Carriageway. The splendid view here includes Lake Awosting. (In the reverse direction, the Long Path drops off the ledge at a sharp left turn in the carriageway). In 25 yards, take the right fork in the carriageway, which twists gently downhill with several splendid views. After following the cliff edge toward a narrowing notch, the road turns away from the edge.

**11.50** A few hundred feet past a sharp switchback turn in the carriageway, the Long Path turns right, goes up two stone steps and enters the woods on a footpath. It soon begins to pass a small ledge on the left. The trail now continues along the edge of Litchfield Ledge, which is separated from Castle Point by a V-shaped cleft that gets progressively wider and deeper. Soon a tremendous view to the south and west opens up. The ledge curves gradually clockwise, and affords views to the north of Lake Awosting and the Catskills as it begins to run above a ravine.

**12.05** Turn left and begin an extremely steep descent into Huntington Ravine. Toward the end, the descent becomes more moderate.

**12.15** Turn right onto the Awosting Lake Carriageway.

**12.60** Turn left, leaving the carriageway, and descend on a footpath. The trail soon crosses a small stream as the forest becomes dominated by hemlock.

**12.80** Rainbow Falls plunges over the opposite cliff wall just after a stream crossing. After the falls, the trail turns right and continues down the valley of Huntington Ravine.

**12.95** The trail turns left and climbs steeply out of the valley. The ascent gradually becomes more gentle as several views appear.

**13.20** Reach the top of a conglomerate rock plane, with a tremendous view to the north. The trail now descends at a moderate pitch down the rock plane, with small pines and blueberries growing in patches of soil on the bare rock. On the way down, the trail briefly passes through better developed woods and crosses a stream. Toward the bottom of the drop, the trail enters scrubby pine woods.

**13.50** Turn right onto the Peters Kill Carriageway (which provides the most direct access to Lake Awosting) and cross the valley of Fly Brook on a causeway. Once over the causeway, the Long Path soon turns left, leaving the carriageway, and follows along a grassy clearing.

**13.65** At the end of the clearing, the trail enters the woods on a slight upgrade and almost immediately turns right onto a wider, rocky trail. The trail begins to follow gentle grades near the top of a gentle slope.

**14.05** The trail crosses a power line right-of-way diagonally to the right. It turns left into the woods at a pair of poles (just before a sharp dropoff), and soon begins to follow near the top of an asymmetrical ridge (gentle to the left, sharp to the right), with occasional views of a parallel ridge across the valley to the right.

**14.70** The Blueberry Run Trail (blue) begins to the right, leading down to the Peters Kill Carriageway. The Long Path soon regains the ridge crest as it passes through short pines.

**14.90** Turn left away from the edge of the ridge and into hardwoods. The trail now descends gently through forest rich in mountain laurel.

**16.50** Cross a stream on rocks.

**16.60** Cross Route 44/55.

**16.75** The trail crosses a stone wall and passes through a grassy field.

**16.80** Reach Jenny Lane, a gravel road (the old Wawarsing Turnpike) (end of section). To continue, turn left and follow the road.

# Section 13

*Jenny Lane (Route 44/55) to*
*Riggsville (Catskill Park)*

---

*Feature*                               *Road Walking*

---

*Distance*                               *12.8 miles*

---

### General description

The first mile of this section is on an old dirt road through
the woods. The rest of the section follows paved roads,
some quite busy, that pass through rural Ulster County
and the Town of Kerhonkson.

### Access

Take the New York State Thruway to Exit 18 (New
Paltz). Continue west on Route 299 through the Town
of New Paltz. At the junction with Route 44/55, go
west (right). About a mile beyond the Minnewaska State
Park parking area on the left and a few hundred yards
past a small stream crossing, turn right on a narrow
gravel access road. Take the first right to the parking
area.

### Parking

**0.0** Parking area at Jenny Lane.
**1.0** End of Shawangunk Drive (limited parking).
**4.1** Street parking in Kerhonkson.
**12.8** DEC parking area at entrance to Catskill Park on
Upper Cherrytown Road.

## Trail description

**0.00** From the end of Section 12 (just north of the parking area), proceed north on Jenny Lane.

**0.10** A gravel road goes left 0.1 mile to Route 44/55. The Long Path continues straight ahead on a dirt road not open to traffic. The general trend is downhill through the forest. At one point, there is a view of the Catskill Mountains.

**1.00** Reach the end of Shawangunk Drive, a gravel road. A few cars can be parked here. The trail continues straight ahead and soon crosses a wooden bridge.

**1.30** The road becomes paved and houses become more frequent.

**1.80** Shawangunk Drive ends at Upper Granite Road (Ulster County Route 27). The trail bears left onto Upper Granite Road.

**2.30** Upper Granite Road ends at Route 44/55 near Dzinban's Country Deli. The trail bears right and follows this busy highway.

**2.80** Pass through an intersection, with the Granite Hotel on the right, and continue down a hill.

**3.40** Where the road flattens out, take the first right since the road to the Granite. This road has a double yellow line (but no sign).

**3.90** Cross Rondout Creek on a steel bridge in Kerhonkson.

**4.10** Cross Route 209 at a traffic light. The VIP Lounge, Stewards Shops, Indian Valley Inn and a gas station are on the corners.

**4.15** At a split in the road, bear left onto a quiet residential road.

**4.40** Cross a small stream.

**4.90** Pass a sign for the Town of Rochester.

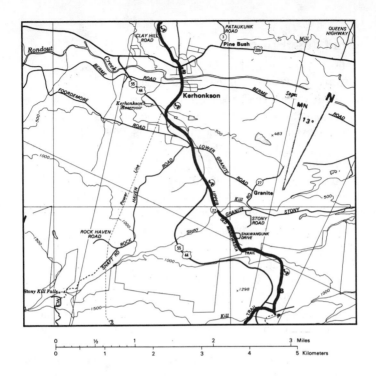

**5.60** Turn left onto Ulster County Route 3, a busy street, soon passing the Shir-Mar-Rae Tavern on the left.

**5.90** Take the first left on an unnamed road, with a sign for the Pinegrove Resort, and go uphill.

**9.50** Pass Baker Road on the left.

**9.60** The trail turns left where the road it has been following ends on another road (Upper Cherrytown Road) that goes straight and left. As the turn is made, houses are on the left and a garage is on the right.

**12.80** The section ends at a Department of Environmental Conservation parking area on the right side of the road. To continue, turn left and enter the woods on a DEC snowmobile trail.

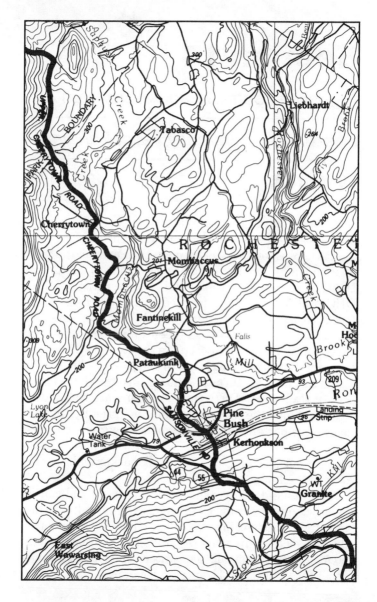

# Section 14

*Riggsville (Catskill Park) to Bull Run*

| | |
|---|---|
| **Features** | *Vernooy Falls, Bangle Hill* |

| | |
|---|---|
| **Distance** | *10.1 miles* |

**The Long Path in the Catskills:** This section marks the beginning of the route of the Long Path through the Catskill Park. Most of its route through the Park follows trails maintained by the Trail Conference for New York State Department of Environmental Conservation (DEC). DEC trails are generally marked with round disks of different colors. These are generally the only markers, and the aqua Long Path blaze is seen only when the Long Path crosses private property. As the Long Path changes frequently from one DEC trail to another, the hiker must watch carefully for turns and make sure that he is on the proper trail. Most DEC trail junctions are marked by signs that give the trail names and the direction and distance to important points (the distances given on these signs are not always precisely accurate). At most of these intersections, a blue Long Path trail marker indicates the route of the Long Path.

The Catskill Park has spectacular scenery and considerable rugged terrain. Camping is permitted on State land at elevations below 3,500 feet (this elevation is usually marked by signs along the trails), at locations at least 150 feet away from trails and water. The Long Path also passes by several DEC leantos and campgrounds.

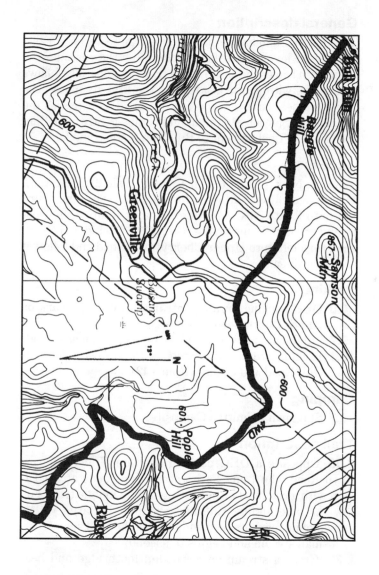

## General description

The Long Path follows a snowmobile trail to Vernooy Falls, a series of lovely waterfalls. Soon after the cascade, the Long Path leaves the snowmobile trail but generally follows dirt roads, with gentle grades, for the first six miles. The trail becomes narrower and more rugged as it passes the shoulder of Samson Mountain and climbs gently over Bangle Hill. The final descent to Bull Run is steep and long.

## Access

Take the New York State Thruway to Exit 19 (Kingston). Continue on Route 28 west for about 3 miles, then turn left onto Route 28A. At Ulster County Route 3, go west to and through Samsonville. Go right on Sundown Road, then turn left onto Upper Cherrytown Road and follow it to the trailhead.

## Parking

**0.0** DEC parking area at entrance to Catskill Park on Upper Cherrytown Road.
**9.7** Sundown Primitive Campsite on Peekamoose Road.
**10.1** Parking area on Peekamoose Road (also known as Gulf Road and County Route 42).

## Camping

**9.7** Sundown Primitive Campsite.

## Trail description

**0.00** Opposite a DEC parking area on Upper Cherrytown Road, the Long Path enters the woods at a DEC sign with a red marker indicating a snowmobile trail. Follow the blue hiking trail markers and the large yellow snowmobile markers on a wide path. The trail soon crosses a small stream and begins to ascend.
**0.25** Cross a stream on a wooden footbridge and bear

right to follow along the stream. In another 0.1 mile, pass a piped spring on the left. The trail soon bears left, away from the stream, and ascends more sharply, as large trees give way to a smaller forest. The trail eventually levels off, and several small streams are crossed.

**1.70** Reach a clearing, with Vernooy Falls—a series of lovely cascades in a large stream—on the left. A number of old foundations are in this area, and the hiker can follow several other paths. The Long Path makes a sharp right turn on a wide cobble path, as it continues to follow the blue trail markers and the yellow markers of the snowmobile trail. After a gradual ascent, the trail becomes generally level and is often wet.

**2.65** The Long Path turns left up a gentle hill as the yellow-marked snowmobile trail continues straight ahead. The Long Path now follows a wide woods road, with blue markers. It soon reaches a gentle hilltop and becomes fairly level.

**3.90** The trail goes left at an intersection of woods roads. It soon crosses a stream on three metal pipe culverts. Several dirt roads lead away from the trail, and a stream approaches from the left and begins to run alongside.

**Vernooy Falls**

**4.60** Cross a tributary stream on a wood plank bridge. The trail passes through hemlock forest before rejoining hardwoods. This section of the trail is often wet.

**5.30** Cross a stream on a metal pipe culvert. In 500 feet, another dirt road goes off to the left.

**5.60** The Long Path goes right on a narrow track, leaving the woods road. The trail climbs, often fairly steeply, until it reaches another woods road. Here it turns left on level ground. (For reverse direction, the turn off this woods road is a few hundred feet before the road curves to the left).

**6.10** At a small crest in the woods road, the Long Path turns right on a footpath, leaving the road. A few hundred yards further on, it makes a sharp left on a well-defined path. The general trend is gently downhill, as several small streams are crossed.

**7.95** The trail jogs left and begins to run along a level grade, with a sharp drop to the right.

**8.65** After reaching the top of Bangle Hill (elevation 2,350 feet), the trail descends steeply, then turns left and continues along a nearly level contour.

**8.85** Cross a rocky intermittent stream, turn right, and head downhill, parallel to the stream. It is now steeply down all the way to the base of Bangle Hill. On the way down the stream is crossed two more times. The trail then crosses the outlet of a spring and continues to follow along the valley of the stream. The trail soon widens into a woods road, and several other woods roads lead left from the trail.

**9.65** Reach Peekamoose Road and turn right, passing a parking area for the Sundown Primitive Campsite on the left. The road is marked by occasional blue paint blazes.

**9.75** Cross bridge over Rondout Creek. In another 600 feet, cross a bridge over a tributary stream.

**10.10** The section ends where the trail leads diagonally uphill on the left side of the road.

# Section 15

*Bull Run to Denning Road*

---

| **Features** | *Peekamoose and Table Mountains* |
|---|---|

---

| **Distance** | *7.6 miles* |
|---|---|

---

## General description

This is a rugged trail section that begins with a three-mile, 2,500-foot ascent of Peekamoose Mountain. Shortly before the top, there is a tremendous view of the Rondout Creek valley. After climbing out of the saddle between Peekamoose and Table Mountains, the trail ascends along the broad, gentle "top" of Table to the summit. From Table, the trail drops to the valley of the East Branch of the Neversink River, where the Denning Lean-to is located. The trail then climbs out of the river valley and joins the Phoenicia-East Branch Trail. For the entire length of the section, the Long Path follows the blue-blazed Peekamoose-Table Trail.

## Access

Take the New York State Thruway to Exit 19 (Kingston). Continue on Route 28 west. In Boiceville, about 17 miles from the Thruway, turn left onto Route 28A. (Do *not* turn left onto Route 28A where it first meets Route 28, about 3 miles west of the Thruway). In West Shokan, turn right onto Peekamoose Road (County Route 42, also known as Gulf Road and as Sundown-West Shokan Road). (This turn may not be marked by a street or route sign, but a large sign points to Grahamville and Town Offices). Follow Peekamoose Road for about 10 miles to a parking area on the right.

## Parking

**0.0** Parking area on Peekamoose Road.
**7.6** Parking area at end of Denning Road (1.2 miles along the Phoenicia-East Branch Trail from the end of this section).

## Camping

**0.0** Sundown Primitive Campsite (on Peekamoose Road, 0.4 mile west of trailhead).
**7.3** Denning Lean-to.

## Trail description

**0.00** From the north side of Peekamoose Road, about 250 feet south of the parking area, the Long Path proceeds uphill on a woods road, following the blue-blazed Peekamoose-Table Trail.

**0.85** The trail turns right, leaving the woods road, and continues on a footpath. The ascent is steady but varying in pitch as the trail alternates between gentle stretches and sharp, rocky climbs.

**2.35** Reach Reconnoiter Rock, a rock outcrop, with a partial view to the northwest. The trail now levels off for some distance.

**3.10** Just past the 3,500-foot elevation sign, reach a wide ledge to the right of the trail, with excellent views. In another 250 feet, an unmaintained trail, with some old red paint blazes, goes off to the right and descends to Peekamoose Road.

**3.35** Pass a spring that comes from a small cleft in the rock to the left, a source of *water*. The trail now passes through a dwarf spruce forest.

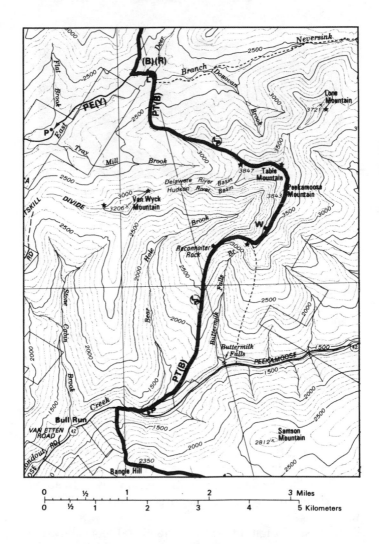

**View from ledge on Peekamoose Mountain**

**3.80** Begin to climb steeply.

**3.95** Reach the summit of Peekamoose Mountain (elevation 3,843 feet), marked by a large rock to the left of the trail. Some views to the northeast are possible from the top of the rock. The trail soon descends steeply into the col between Peekamoose and Table Mountains.

**4.20** Reach the base of the col, and begin gentle ascent.

**4.40** Begin a steep ascent up Table Mountain. The grade soon moderates, then becomes extremely gentle when the nearly flat ridge of Table Mountain is attained. Shortly after attaining the ridge, an unmarked trail to the right leads to an excellent viewpoint over the Burroughs Range and Rocky and Lone Mountains to the northeast.

**4.80** Reach the summit of Table Mountain, on the divide between the drainage basins of the Hudson and Delaware Rivers. (The wooded summit affords no views). Descend, sometimes steeply, as spruce forest is replaced by hardwoods.

**5.15** Pass a sign indicating the 3,500-foot elevation.

In another 400 feet, a faint side trail leads, right, about 50 feet to an unreliable spring, a possible source of *water*.

**5.55** Begin to climb over a small knoll. The way down includes four sharp drops that are separated by gentler sections.

**6.35** The descent is interrupted briefly by a second small knoll.

**7.20** The trail drops into the broad, flat flood plain of the East Branch of the Neversink River.

**7.30** Pass the Denning Lean-to on the right. The lean-to is situated in a wonderfully picturesque setting amidst the multiple channels of the East Branch of the Neversink. Beyond the lean-to, two new log bridges have been constructed across Deer Shanty Brook where crossings at times of high water were formerly a problem.

**7.45** Climb out of the flood plain and ascend gently.

**7.60** Reach the yellow-blazed Phoenicia-East Branch Trail (end of section). To continue, turn right and follow the yellow markers. To the left, it is 1.2 miles to the parking area at the end of Denning Road.

**At the summit of Peekamoose Mountain**

# Section 16

*Denning Road to Woodland Valley*

| | |
|---|---|
| ***Features*** | *Slide, Cornell and Wittenberg Mountains* |

| | |
|---|---|
| ***Distance*** | *11.15 miles* |

## General description

From the valley of the East Branch of the Neversink River, the Long Path follows the route of the Phoenicia-East Branch Trail. At the Curtis Monument, it turns onto the ridge of the Burroughs Range. Slide Mountain, the first encountered on the ridge, is the highest peak in the Catskills. The trail then passes over Cornell and Wittenberg Mountains before dropping to Woodland Valley. Since several DEC trails are followed by the Long Path in this section, the hiker should be careful at trail junctions to choose the correct trail (changes in color of trail blazes are noted in the text in boldface type).

## Access

***From New York City:*** Take the New York State Thruway to Exit 16 (Harriman). Continue on Route 17 west to Exit 100 (Liberty). Turn left at the end of the exit ramp, and go to the first traffic light. Turn left onto Route 52 west. Follow Route 52 for one mile, then turn right onto Route 55 east. Continue on Route 55 for 10 miles to Curry. At a sign on the right for Claryville, turn left onto County Route 19 (Denning Road) and follow it for 13 miles to the trailhead at the end of the road. (After about

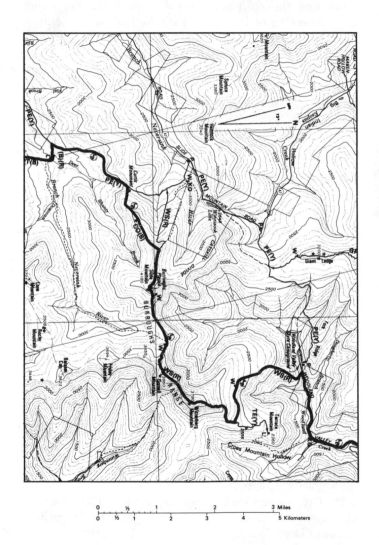

7.5 miles, the designation of the road as a county road ends, and the road narrows). To reach the beginning of this section of the Long Path, follow the Phoenicia-East Branch Trail northeast from the parking area for 1.2 miles.

*From the Hudson Valley:* Take the New York State Thruway to Exit 18 (New Paltz). Continue west on Route 299 through the Town of New Paltz. At the junction with Route 44/55, go west (right). Follow Route 55 to Curry, and make a right onto County Route 19. Continue as described above.

## Parking

**0.0** Parking area at end of Denning Road (1.2 miles along the Phoenicia-East Branch Trail from the beginning of this section).

**11.2** Woodland Valley State Campground (parking fee charged in season).

## Camping

**8.6** Terrace Mountain Lean-to (0.9 mile from the Long Path on yellow-blazed Terrace Mountain Trail; no water).

**11.2** Woodland Valley State Campground (fee charged).

## Trail description

**0.00** From the intersection of the Peekamoose-Table Trail with the Phoenicia-East Branch Trail, proceed north on the **yellow**-blazed Phoenicia-East Branch Trail (a woods road). The trail rises gently but steadily through hardwood forest, crossing a few small streams.

**0.55** Pass spring to the left of the trail.

**0.85** Cross a stream on a wooden bridge. The trail soon runs along the shoulder of a steep slope, with the rushing water of Deer Shanty Brook below to the right.

**1.75** Turn right onto the **blue**-blazed Curtis-Ormsbee Trail. (The yellow-blazed Phoenicia-East Branch Trail continues straight ahead, reaching County Route 47 in 1.5 miles). Near the junction is a stone monument in memory of William ("Father Bill") Curtis and Allen Ormsbee, both of whom died in a snowstorm on Mt. Washington on June 30, 1900. (The trail is named in their memory). The Curtis-Ormsbee Trail leads up the ridge of the Burroughs Range, which comes into view just before the trail junction. The ascent is sometimes steeply up rock ledges, and alternates between hardwood and spruce forest.

**2.40** About 500 feet past the sign marking the 3,500-foot elevation, a short side trail leads, right, to a ledge with a spectacular lookout. Table Mountain (with its long, flat top) and Rocky and Lone Mountains are clearly visible. The ascent continues, with both level, swampy stretches and steep climbs.

**3.40** Turn right onto the **red**-blazed Wittenberg-Cornell-Slide Trail. The trail ascends gently through dense spruce trees.

**At the summit of Slide Mountain**

**4.05** Reach the summit of Slide Mountain (marked by a concrete slab—a remnant of a former fire tower). At 4,180 feet in elevation, this is the highest point in the Catskill Mountains. In another 300 feet, an outcrop on the left side of the trail offers an excellent view to the east, with the Ashokan Reservoir visible in the distance below. The Burroughs Plaque, commemorating John Burroughs, is set into the side of this outcrop. The descent from Slide is steep and rugged, with wooden steps provided in the steepest section. Several good views are possible along the way.

**4.30** A sign marks the way to a spring—a dependable source of *water*—on the left side of the trail. The pitch of the descent soon becomes more moderate, but several sharp rock faces must be traversed.

**5.00** Reach the low spot between Slide and Cornell Mountain. An unmarked trail leads, right, about 300 feet to a spring. (This is a popular camping spot for those doing the Wittenberg-Cornell-Slide circular). Beyond the col, the trail levels off and soon passes around a wet area. In the spring, the hobblebush puts on a spectacular show in this area. Soon the trail begins to ascend Cornell Mountain, passing through a dense spruce-balsam forest. As the trail nears the summit of Cornell, it climbs steeply over a series of rock ledges.

**6.25** Reach the top of a rock ledge. To the left of the trail is a rock outcropping with a spectacular view of the great Panther-Slide Wilderness Area—the largest unbroken land mass in the Catskills. Views of Slide Mountain and the its slide are directly ahead. To the left, Peekamoose, Table, Lone and Rocky Mountains are visible. To the right of Slide are Giant Ledge and Panther Mountain, with the Devil's Path range in the far distance. From this viewpoint, there is no evidence of civilization in the Catskills.

**6.45** To the right, a short yellow-blazed side trail leads to the summit of Cornell Mountain (elevation 3,860 feet).

The view from Cornell is somewhat overgrown, but there are good views eastward to the Ashokan Reservoir. From here, the trail begins to descend.

**6.55** The trail reaches the top of a rock ledge, with a view to the northwest towards Wittenberg Mountain. The trail scrambles down a very steep crevice in the rock ledge. It soon begins to follow the "Bruin's Causeway"— the path along the ridge between Cornell and Wittenberg. This is one of the highest cols in the Catskills, with the elevation remaining over 3,500 feet.

**6.90** Reach the col between Cornell and Wittenberg Mountains. To the right, a faint old trail leads down extremely steeply to Moon Haw Road in Maltby Hollow. This trail should be avoided by all but the most experienced hikers. The Long Path now begins its climb to the summit of Wittenberg Mountain.

**7.25** Reach the summit of Wittenberg Mountain (elevation 3,780 feet), with a large open rock ledge which affords a tremendous view to the east. The Ashokan Reservoir is visible down below, with Ashokan High Point be-

**Wittenberg Mountain**

yond. On a clear day, the Hudson River may be seen in the distance, with the Taconic Mountains (at the Connecticut-Massachusetts border) far beyond. To the north, the Devil's Path range is visible. The trail soon begins a steep descent over a series of rock ledges, continuing through the characteristic spruce-balsam summit forest.

**8.15** The Long Path begins to level off and now follows a trail that was constructed by the CCC. It passes through a high elevation deciduous forest.

**8.55** The Long Path turns left, following the red-blazed Wittenberg-Cornell-Slide Trail, as the yellow-blazed Terrace Mountain Trail continues straight, reaching the Terrace Mountain Lean-to in 0.9 mile. This trail once continued down to Woodland Valley Road, and was the original route up Wittenberg Mountain from the north, but the part beyond the lean-to was abandoned when the present route of the Wittenberg-Cornell-Slide Trail was constructed from the Woodland Valley Campground. The Wittenberg-Cornell-Slide Trail soon dips slightly to cross a small stream and then levels off as it follows the northern shoulder of Wittenberg Mountain.

**9.70** The trail passes a spring about 300 feet to the left of the trail, where water flows over a rock ledge. Shortly beyond the spring, the trail begins to descend more steeply. After one steep section, the trail passes through a hemlock grove, with a view from a ledge to the right over Woodland Valley. The trail continues to descend through a series of boulders, levels off for a short distance, and then makes its final descent to Woodland Valley.

**11.05** After passing a register box, the trail crosses Woodland Creek on a wooden bridge.

**11.15** Reach Woodland Valley Road (end of section). To the left, there is a large parking area. The DEC charges a fee to park here (in season). To continue, turn right and follow Woodland Valley Road eastward.

# Section 17

*Woodland Valley to Phoenicia*

| | |
|---|---|
| ***Feature*** | *Road Walking* |

| | |
|---|---|
| ***Distance*** | *5.75 miles* |

### General description

The Long Path follows paved roads in this section. The trail runs along Woodland Creek much of the way through a narrow, mountainous corridor. After Woodland Creek intersects Esopus Creek, the trail continues east along Esopus Creek, and soon crosses the Esopus into the Village of Phoenicia.

### Access

Take the New York State Thruway to Exit 19 (Kingston). Follow Route 28 west for 23 miles to Phoenicia. Turn right at the second turn to Phoenicia (Bridge Street). Follow Bridge Street to just before the railroad tracks, and turn left onto High Street. Follow High Street and then Woodland Valley Road 5.5 miles to the Woodland Valley State Campground.

### Parking

**0.0** Woodland Valley State Campground (parking fee charged in season).

**5.8** Village of Phoenicia (parking available on Main Street or behind the Phoenicia Pharmacy on Route 214).

## Camping

**0.0** Woodland Valley State Campground (fee charged).

## Trail description

**0.00** From the Woodland Valley State Campground, proceed eastward on Woodland Valley Road.

**1.30** Pass old swinging suspension bridge to the right. This was the original route of the Wittenberg-Cornell-Slide Trail (and Long Path) over Terrace Mountain, but was abandoned some years ago when the private landowner along the creek closed the trail.

**2.10** Pass Fawn Hill on the left.

**3.85** Cross Panther Kill.

**4.20** Cross Woodland Creek.

**4.60** Herdman Road comes in from the left. Continue straight ahead.

**4.70** To the left, an old bridge (now closed to vehicular traffic) crosses Esopus Creek. The Long Path continues ahead on High Street, which runs parallel to Esopus Creek. It soon crosses under Route 28 and intersects Bridge Street.

**5.60** The Long Path turns left on Bridge Street, crosses the railroad tracks and then Esopus Creek, and enters Phoenicia. The railroad tracks—formerly the route of the Ulster and Delaware Railroad—are now operated by a local tourist short-line, the Catskill Mountain Railroad. The Ulster and Delaware once brought trainloads of tourists to this portion of the Catskills. Today, the Catskill Mountain Railroad ferries tubers from Mt. Pleasant to Phoenicia.

**5.75** Reach Main Street in Phoenicia (County Route 40) (end of section). To the left is the center of Phoenicia. While just two blocks long, it is well worth the detour. It is home of several restaurants and a number of antique

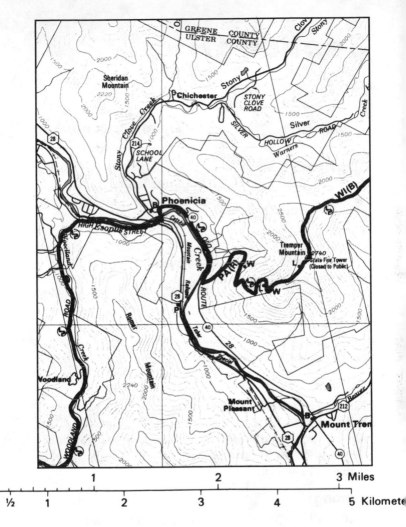

shops. There is also a grocery store and general store here for backpackers to resupply. To continue on the Long Path, turn right and proceed eastward on Main Street (County Route 40).

# Section 18

*Phoenicia to Lake Hill*

| | |
|---|---|
| ***Feature*** | *Tremper Mountain* |

| | |
|---|---|
| ***Distance*** | *11.4 miles* |

## General description

The Long Path leaves Phoenicia on public roads, paralleling the Esopus Creek. The trail then climbs up the south side of Tremper Mountain, following an old tote road to the former state fire tower. North of the fire tower the blazes change color, and the Long Path descends to the hamlet of Willow on a little used trail which follows the ridge towards Carl Mountain in the north and then descends to Hoyt Hollow. Beyond Willow, the trail follows public roads for the rest of the section.

## Access

Take the New York State Thruway to Exit 19 (Kingston). Follow Route 28 west for 23 miles to Phoenicia. Turn right at the second turn to Phoenicia (Bridge Street). Follow Bridge Street across the Esopus Creek to Main Street in Phoenicia.

## Parking

**0.0** Village of Phoenicia (parking available on Main Street or behind the Phoenicia Pharmacy on Route 214).

**8.9** Willow Post Office.

**11.4** Mink Hollow Road and Route 212 at Lake Hill.

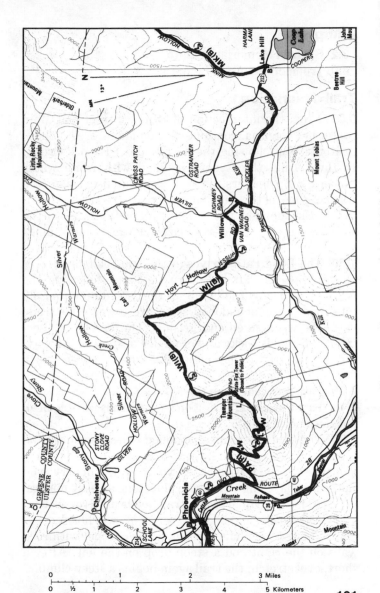

## Camping

**3.2** Baldwin Memorial Lean-to.
**4.0** Tremper Mountain Lean-to.

## Trail description

**0.00** From the intersection of Bridge Street and Main Street in Phoenicia, continue east on Main Street (County Route 40), following the north side of Esopus Creek. In the spring, the Esopus is filled with white water canoers and kayakers, as well as trout fishermen (the Esopus is one of the most famous trout streams in America). In the summer, the primary recreational use of the creek is by people who ride lazily downstream in inner tubes.

**1.30** The Long Path arrives at the trailhead of the red-blazed Phoenicia Trail. It turns left and, following the red blazes, begins the climb up the mountain on an old tote road to the abandoned state fire tower. The grade varies between steep and gradual. On the steeper sections, the trail is rocky and eroded. For most of the way, the trail passes through a mixed hardwood and hemlock forest.

**2.05** Pass rock ledges on the left

**2.15** Pass a seasonal spring on left, which is reliable in all but the driest times.

**2.20** The trail passes an abandoned bluestone quarry on the left. Bluestone mining was once one of the primary industries in the Catskills. As you pass the quarry, you can see the layering that made bluestone an easy mineral to mine. Past the quarry the trail levels off, crosses several woods roads, and begins a series of switchbacks.

**2.95** The trail sidehills through a steep slope, with rock walls on the right and a steep drop on the left. After a short level stretch, the trail again begins a steep climb.

**3.15** A side trail to the right leads to the Baldwin Memorial Lean-to. In another 250 feet, pass an undependable pipe spring 50 feet to the left of the trail.

**3.65** After a switchback, the trail climbs to the top of the ridge, which it follows the rest of the way to the summit. Here the forest is less mature; consequently, there is more undergrowth.

**4.00** Pass the Tremper Mountain Lean-to on the left.

**4.05** Reach the flat, level summit of Mt. Tremper, with an abandoned state fire tower, formerly used by fire observers with two-way radios. These towers were placed on top of selected mountains in the early 1900's after a series of fires devastated the mountains. More recently, the fire towers have been replaced by aircraft patrols. *Do not climb the tower*! To the right of the tower is an open area which affords a view of the Devil's Path when the leaves are down. Continuing past the tower, the Long Path passes through a cleared area and then begins to descend, now following the blue-blazed Willow Trail. It passes through a fairly open forest, with a base of blackberry brambles.

**4.30** The trail enters a more mature forest, with little undergrowth. It continues to descend along the ridge top towards the col between Tremper Mountain and Carl Mountain. Initially, the trail follows the eastern slope of the ridge, with seasonal views through the trees over the Devil's Path to the north.

**4.95** The trail levels out and the begins a gradual climb of the north peak of Tremper Mountain. For the most part, the trail stays about 200 vertical feet below the top of the ridge, following the western slopes.

**5.80** After passing through a hemlock grove, the trail descends along the eastern side of the ridge.

**6.10** Reach the col between Tremper Mountain and Carl Mountain. Here, the trail turns right, leaving the ridge, and descends steeply into Hoyt Hollow, following along the state land boundary.

**6.40**  The trail levels off for a short distance and sidehills through a very steep section of the mountain. Soon, the trail begins to follow an old woods road.

**7.10**  The trail now leaves state land and enters private property. Please stay on the trail in this section. Continue to descend, sometimes steeply, crossing a series of old, grassy woods roads.

**7.65**  Turn right onto gravel Jessup Road (passable by car), and continue to descend through an area of hemlocks and white pines. Soon the trail passes a house on the left, with a car turnaround on the right (do not park here).

**7.95**  After passing several houses, Jessup Road becomes paved. There is an incorrect trail signpost here on the left, with a sign to Willow Farm on the right. The trail continues to follow paved Jessup Road.

**8.75**  Turn right onto Van Wagner Road. In another 500 feet, pass the Willow post office on the left.

**9.00**  Turn right onto Route 212. Here the trail markings change from blue DEC markers to aqua Long Path paint blazes.

**9.15**  Turn left onto Sickler Road. The walk along Sickler Road is pleasantly rural, passing a number of houses along the way. The middle section is forested, as a ridge from Mount Tobias comes down to the road.

**11.05**  Turn right onto Route 212.

**11.40**  Reach Mink Hollow Road in Lake Hill (end of section). To continue, turn left onto Mink Hollow Road.

# Section 19

*Lake Hill to Platte Clove Road*

| | |
|---|---|
| ***Features*** | *Sugarloaf and Twin Mountains* |

| | |
|---|---|
| ***Distance*** | *12.5 miles* |

## General description

This section of the Long Path begins and ends with two short road walks. In between is some of the most spectacular and rugged scenery in the Catskills. The trail begins by following paved Mink Hollow Road. When the pavement ends, Mink Hollow Road continues as a woods road to Mink Hollow. This part of the trip passes through pleasant forest lands, and the climb is gentle to moderate. At Mink Hollow, all this changes, as the Long Path begins to follows the Devil's Path over Sugarloaf and Twin Mountains. This trail climbs and descends in dramatic fashion, clambering over and through large rock ledges. Both mountains offer excellent views. After descending Twin Mountain, the section ends with a roadwalk on Prediger and Platte Clove Roads. Since several DEC trails are followed by the Long Path in this section, the hiker should be careful at trail junctions to choose the correct trail (changes in color of trail blazes are noted in the text in boldface type).

## Access

Take the New York State Thruway to Exit 20 (Saugerties). Take Route 212 west through the hamlet of Woodstock. Beyond Woodstock, continue on Route 212 to Mink Hollow Road in Lake Hill.

## Parking

**0.0** Mink Hollow Road and Route 212 at Lake Hill.

**2.8** End of paved Mink Hollow Road.

**12.5** On the south side of Platte Clove Road, about 100 feet east of the bridge to the east of the snowmobile trail.

## Camping

**5.4** Mink Hollow Lean-to.

## Trail description

**0.00** From the intersection of Route 212 and Mink Hollow Road, the Long Path proceeds north on paved Mink Hollow Road, following the **blue** DEC markers of the Mink Hollow Trail. For the first 2.8 miles, Mink Hollow Road is a paved road, but it is rural in character, with a mix of homes and forested lands. The Beaver Kill (different from the famous trout stream in the southern Catskills) flows out of Mink Hollow and initially parallels the road on the left side.

**1.25** Cross the Beaver Kill. The stream now runs along the right side of the road.

**1.80** Van Hoagland Road goes off to the right. The trail continues ahead on Mink Hollow Road.

**2.10** A small slide is visible on the mountainside across the Beaver Kill to the right.

**2.60** A cinder road goes off to the left. The trail continues ahead on Mink Hollow Road.

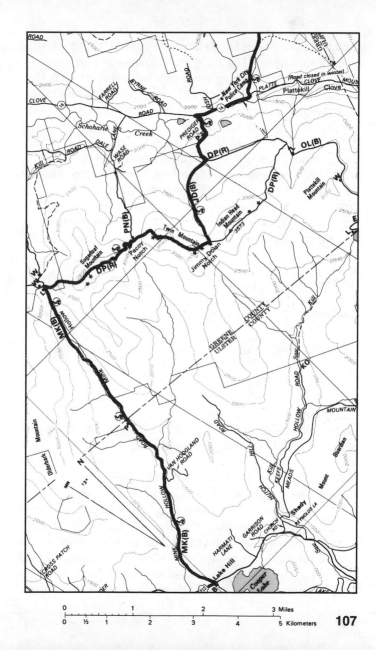

**2.80** The paved road ends at a turnaround (there is room to park cars here). The Long Path turns right on a woods road (an old 19th century mountain turnpike, which is the continuation of Mink Hollow Road), following the blue-blazed Mink Hollow Trail. It soon passes the last few houses and enters state land.

**3.15** Cross the Beaver Kill. The trail continues along the woods road, passing through a deciduous forest.

**3.30** The trail crosses a state land boundary and enters the Plateau-Indian Head Wilderness Area.

**3.80** The trail turns left and recrosses the Beaver Kill. An abutment along the stream bank is a remnant of an old bridge. Soon the trail begins a moderate climb towards Mink Hollow.

**4.15** Cross a small tributary stream.

**4.60** The trail levels off as it crosses several small streams. It soon resumes its ascent.

**4.90** The trail begins its final steep ascent to Mink Hollow.

**5.20** The trail levels off and soon begins a slight downgrade.

**5.35** Pass the Mink Hollow Lean-to on the left.

**5.40** Reach the col between Plateau and Sugarloaf Mountains in Mink Hollow. The Long Path turns right onto the **red**-blazed Devil's Path and begins its steep ascent up Sugarloaf Mountain, as the blue-blazed Mink Hollow Trail continues straight ahead on a woods road that descends to Elka Park to the north. The Devil's Path is the most dramatic trail in the Catskills, going up and over six major peaks. As its name implies, there are tremendous dropoffs between the peaks. A hike of the entire Devil's Path (west-to-east) involves a gain of over 8,000 feet in total elevation—an elevation gain comparable to that of the Great Range in the Adirondacks!

**5.55** The trail passes two large rocks on the left and soon

**Descending Sugarloaf Mountain in winter**

reaches the first of a series of five rock ledges that the trail climbs over. After passing under a natural bridge in the rock ledge and ascending very steeply, the trail passes a large rock on the right (which contains a natural shelter) and ascends to a second rock ledge, with huge overhangs. The trail then makes a sharp switchback, climbs very steeply over the ledge, and continues steeply uphill.

**5.95** The forest becomes primarily balsam fir and red spruce, with birch mixed in, as the grade begins to moderate.

**6.15** Pass the sign indicating the 3,500-foot elevation. The forest now becomes more open, with views to the left of the Blackhead Range to the north. The trail soon passes a large rock on the right, with excellent views of Plateau Mountain and Mink Hollow.

**6.35** A yellow-blazed side trail to the right leads to a rock ledge, with an outstanding view of the southern Catskills. Visible are the Burroughs Range, Giant Ledge and Panther Mountain, and the mountains along the Pine

Hill-West Branch Trail. The Ashokan Reservoir can also be seen, with the Shawangunks in the background. On a clear day, you can see all the way to the Hudson River valley.

**6.40** Reach the flat, level summit of Sugarloaf Mountain (elevation 3,800 feet). To the right, another yellow-blazed trail leads to an somewhat overgrown viewpoint to the south. The trail continues ahead through a mature balsam-spruce forest, soon beginning to descend in a series of steps, alternating with level sections.

**7.00** Reach a viewpoint to the east over Pecoy Notch, with Twin and Overlook Mountains visible beyond, and the Ashokan Reservoir and the Shawangunks in the distance. The trail now begins a very steep descent into Pecoy Notch.

**7.15** Descend steeply over a series of rock ledges, with many good views over Pecoy Notch and towards Twin Mountain.

**7.60** The trail reaches Pecoy Notch, the col between Sugarloaf and Twin Mountains. To the left, the blue-

**View from Sugarloaf Mountain**

blazed Pecoy Notch Trail descends to Wase Road and Platte Clove Road. The Long Path continues straight ahead and begins a very steep climb of Twin Mountain, climbing over large rocks and several rock ledges.

**7.80** Pass a huge rock on the left that separated from the main ledge.

**7.95** The trail goes through a narrow passage and climbs up a rock ledge.

**8.15** Reach a rock ledge with a large overhanging rock (which provides shelter) on the left. The trail continues straight ahead through a cleft in the rock ledge. At the top of the ledge, there is a good viewpoint, with Sugarloaf Mountain and the fire tower on Hunter Mountain visible to the west, and the Blackhead Range, Stoppel Point and Roundtop visible to the north. The grade now moderates.

**8.30** The trail turns left and climbs a small ledge to reach a viewpoint at the north or true summit of Twin Mountain (elevation 3,640 feet). From this vantage point, one can see Sugarloaf, Plateau and Hunter Mountains to the west, the Burroughs Range to the south, and the Ashokan Reservoir and the Shawangunk Mountains to the southeast, with the Hudson Valley and the Hudson Highlands far in the distance. (The actual summit of Twin is slightly beyond this viewpoint). The trail now descends through a mature spruce-balsam forest.

**8.60** Reach the col between the two peaks of Twin Mountain. The trail now ascends gradually to the south peak of Twin.

**8.95** Reach the south peak of Twin Mountain, with an excellent 180° view. To the west, Sugarloaf and Plateau Mountains are visible, and to the south all the major peaks of the southern Catskills may be seen. To the southeast, the Ashokan Reservoir and the Shawangunks are visible, with the Hudson Highlands and the Hudson Valley in the distance. Overlook Mountain may be seen to the east, with the Hudson River and the Taconics in the far distance. This is one of the best views in the Catskills. The south peak of Twin, while over 3,500 feet high, is not considered as a separate peak by the Catskill 3500 Club, since the drop between the north and south peaks of Twin is less than the required 200 feet. The trail continues eastward, soon beginning to descend.

**9.05** Reach a viewpoint to the east over Jimmy Dolan Notch and Indian Head Mountain. The trail now begins to descend more steeply.

**9.20** Descend over a rock ledge and pass under a large balanced rock to the left.

**9.35** The trail reaches Jimmy Dolan Notch, the col between Twin and Indian Head Mountains. This notch has the highest elevation of all the cols along the Devil's Path, so the climbs to the adjacent mountains are shorter. (As you head west on the Devil's Path, each successive notch is deeper). The Long Path turns left and descends steeply along the **blue**-blazed Jimmy Dolan Notch Trail, as the red-blazed Devil's Path continues ahead over Indian Head Mountain.

**Jimmy Dolan Notch**

**9.65** The trail bears to the right as the grade moderates, and soon crosses several small streams.

**9.95** Enter a hemlock grove, and continue through a hemlock forest.

**10.45** The trail emerges on a woods road and continues downhill.

**10.85** After crossing Schoharie Creek, the Jimmy Dolan Notch Trail ends at its second intersection with the Devil's Path. (The Devil's Path comes in from the right after crossing the summit of Indian Head Mountain, descending to Devil's Kitchen and then switching back under the northern slopes of Indian Head). The Long Path turns left and continues along the **red**-blazed Devil's Path, following the woods road parallel to Schoharie Creek.

**11.15** Pass the trailhead register box.

**11.30** Cross a tributary of Schoharie Creek on a wooden bridge and emerge at a parking area at the end of Prediger Road. (There is a private home adjacent to the trailhead; please respect the privacy of the landowner and do not block the turnaround at the end of the road). The Long Path continues along paved Prediger Road.

**11.70** The trail reaches Platte Clove Road and turns right.

**12.10** On the left is a large lodge that is the home of the Hutterian Brethren. This building was formerly known as the New York City Police Camp.

**12.35** A trail, marked with green metal markers, goes off to the right, crosses the stream and follows the old Overlook Mountain Road into Devil's Kitchen, where it joins the Devil's Path. This green-blazed trail passes through lands of the Catskill Center, which maintains the trail. The Long Path continues ahead on Platte Clove Road.

**12.50** The Kaaterskill High Peak Snowmobile Trail leaves to the left (end of section). To continue, turn left and follow the snowmobile trail.

# Section 20

*Platte Clove Road to Palenville*

| | |
|---|---|
| ***Features*** | *Buttermilk and Wildcat Falls* |
| ***Distance*** | *10.0 miles* |

## General description

The first part of this section runs along a DEC snowmobile trail which ascends the northern slopes of Kaaterskill High Peak on rather gentle grades. After leaving the snowmobile trail, the Long Path descends gradually at first and then steeply to the old Red Gravel Hill Road, which it follows the rest of the way. For the next two miles it is level, passing a series of dramatic waterfalls with a spectacular view into Kaaterskill Clove. After a brief ascent, it descends continuously into Palenville, passing a number of abandoned bluestone quarries. For most of this section, the Long Path is marked by blue DEC trail markers. The last part of the section, which crosses private property, is marked by aqua paint blazes.

## Access

Take the New York State Thruway to Exit 20 (Saugerties). Continue on Route 212 west to the small town of Circleville. As Route 212 curves to the left, bear right onto Ulster County Route 35. Shortly after passing the Blue Mountain Campground, Route 35 makes a sharp left turn. Turn left here, but soon afterwards continue straight ahead on Ulster County Route 33 as Route 35 turns right. In about two miles, the road (now known as Platte Clove Mountain Road) turns into a dramatic moun-

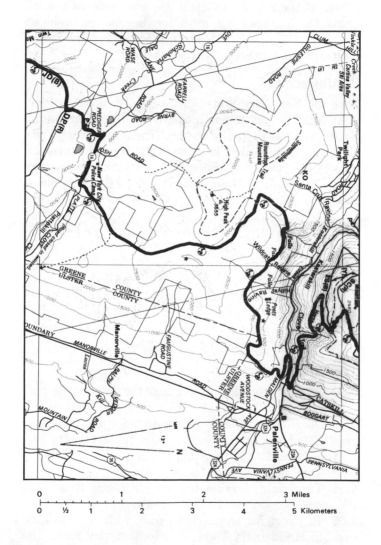

| 0 | | 1 | | 2 | | 3 Miles |
| 0 | ½ | 1 | 2 | 3 | 4 | 5 Kilometers |

115

tain road that climbs over 1,000 feet in less than three miles. At the top of the climb, the road crosses a small brook; the trailhead is immediately beyond the brook on the right. *Platte Clove Mountain Road is closed in the winter; for alternate access, see below.*

## Winter access

Take the New York State Thruway to Exit 20 (Saugerties). Take Route 32 north to Route 32A. Continue on Route 32A north to Palenville. Turn left (west) onto Route 23A, and follow it through Kaaterskill Clove and past Haines Falls to Tannersville. In Tannersville, turn left at the traffic light and continue along Greene County Route 16 (known for most of the way as Platte Clove Road) to the top of Platte Clove. The trailhead is on the left, just before the stream crossing.

## Parking

**0.0** On the south side of Platte Clove Road, about 100 feet east of the bridge to the east of the trailhead.

**9.4** On the north side of Malden Avenue, about 100 feet beyond where Route 23A joins this road (the road is barricaded to vehicular traffic beyond this point).

## Trail description

**0.00** From Platte Clove Road, take the snowmobile trail to the north, following the old Steenburg Road uphill. The snowmobile trail is blazed with large orange or yellow DEC plastic snowmobile markers (in addition to blue DEC markers for the Long Path).

**0.70** Turn right onto another dirt road.

**0.95** Turn right, leaving the old Steenburg Road, and follow another old woods road northward.

**1.05** To the right, an unofficial trail, with red markers, leads to Huckleberry Point, an excellent viewpoint. The

Long Path continues straight ahead on nearly level grades.

**1.35** Cross bridges over a pair of streams in a swampy area. After the second bridge, the ascent resumes, as the trail climbs to the 3,000-foot elevation on the north flank of Kaaterskill High Peak.

**2.25** Reach the highest point on the trail in this section in an area known as the "Pine Plains." The trail continues through nearly level—though swampy—terrain. For the next 0.75 mile, the forest is typical of that found at higher elevations, with considerable spruce, hemlock and birch.

**3.50** The snowmobile trail turns left, uphill, while the Long Path, blazed with blue DEC markers, continues straight ahead. (To climb Kaaterskill High Peak, turn left with the snowmobile trail, turn right in 0.1 mile onto the snowmobile loop trail, then soon turn left onto an unofficial blue-blazed trail which leads to the summit of High Peak). The Long Path now goes through drier terrain.

**3.70** The Long Path turns right (north) onto an old trail that formerly ran from the private community of Twilight Park to High Peak, and begins to descend off the ridge. The descent is often steep and contains many small switchbacks.

**4.15** Leave the old Twilight Park Trail and begin to descend over a series of sharp slopes and narrow flat ledges.

**4.80** The trail reaches another narrow ledge, turns right on the old Red Gravel Hill Road, and begins to run parallel to the edge of the great drop to Kaaterskill Clove on the left.

**5.00** Reach Buttermilk Falls (just to the left of the trail), a spectacular two-step waterfall. Cross the stream and continue along level ledge.

**5.50** Reach Wildcat Falls, another spectacular waterfall. The ledge to the west of the falls affords an excellent view of Kaaterskill Clove and the Hudson Valley to the east. Cross the stream and continue along the level trail. Soon

**Kaaterskill Clove**

you will descend a small ledge to the left, pass a large boulder, and bear right along the slope edge again.

**6.00** Cross the two streams of Hillyer Ravine, which provide the last sure source of *water* in this section. The trail now ascends slightly and crosses several intermittent streams.

**6.95** Reach the crest of the rise and begin to descend. The trail continues downhill—at times, steeply—until reaching Malden Avenue. The trail uses several long switchbacks in its descent, and an old bluestone quarry is passed to the right of the trail.

**8.50** Cross the state land boundary. Since the Long Path now runs over private property, the trail markers change from blue DEC plastic markers to aqua paint blazes.

**8.95** Reach Malden Avenue in Palenville and turn left along the road.

**9.45** After going around a barricade which blocks vehicular traffic, turn right onto Route 23A.

**10.00** The section ends where the Sleepy Hollow Horse Trail leaves to the left, just east of an "Entering Catskill Park" sign. To continue, turn left onto the horse trail.

# Section 21

*Palenville to North Lake*

| | |
|---|---|
| ***Features*** | *Kaaterskill Clove and North Lake* |
| ***Distance*** | *4.8 miles* |

## General description

For most of this section, the Long Path follows the Sleepy Hollow Horse Trail, the route of the old Harding Road which led from Palenville to the Hotel Kaaterskill. There are a number of views along this route, which is blazed with the yellow markers of the horse trail. The Kaaterskill Clove Lookout provides a dramatic open view of the clove, and there are continuous views of the clove through the trees when the leaves are down. Upon reaching the Escarpment, the Long Path follows the blue-blazed Escarpment Trail, passing the sites of the two most famous nineteenth century hotels in the Catskills—the Hotel Kaaterskill and the Catskill Mountain House. Along the way, there are several spectacular views of Kaaterskill Clove and the Hudson Valley. The section ends at North Lake, once used for recreation by guests of the Catskill Mountain House. Today, it is the site of a large state campground, complete with a beach and a boat rental facility.

## Access

Take the New York State Thruway to Exit 20 (Saugerties). Take Route 32 north to Route 32A. Continue on

Route 32A north to Palenville. Turn left (west) onto Route 23A, and pass through the Village of Palenville. The section begins a short distance beyond the village, about 100 feet east of an "Entering Catskill Park" sign, where the Long Path enters the woods on the Sleepy Hollow Horse Trail.

## Parking

**0.0** On Route 23A, about 0.4 mile west of the "Entering Catskill Park" sign, there is a small parking area on the north side of the road, just before the bridge over Kaaterskill Creek.

**4.8** North Lake State Campground, at North Lake Beach (parking fee charged in season).

## Camping

**4.8** North Lake State Campground (fee charged).

## Trail description

**0.00** From Route 23A, about 100 feet east of the "Entering Catskill Park" sign, the Long Path proceeds north, following the yellow-blazed Sleepy Hollow Horse Trail—the route of the old Harding Road from Palenville to the Hotel Kaaterskill. Shortly after leaving Route 23A, the trail switchbacks to the left and begins a long climb up Kaaterskill Clove. The trail parallels the clove most of the way, climbing 1,400 feet in three miles.

**0.25** A woods road goes off to the right. The Long Path continues ahead on the Sleepy Hollow Horse Trail.

**0.55** The trail enters state land and soon passes a talus slope on the right.

**0.95** Reach a trail register. Here the trail turns right and follows a deep side gorge formed by a stream. Just past the register, the trail reaches Kaaterskill Clove Lookout, which affords a spectacular view to the left into

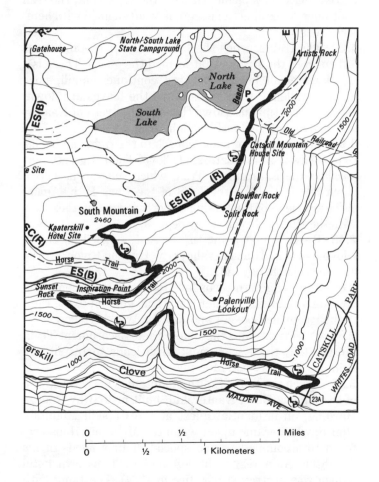

Kaaterskill Clove. Kaaterskill High Peak towers over the clove on the south side. On the right side of the trail, there is a stone fireplace below a small rock ledge. This is a great place for a picnic. Beyond the viewpoint, the trail continues to parallel the gorge, now often lined with hemlock trees.

**1.20** The trail reaches the head of the gorge and turns left to cross the stream that formed the gorge. There is a small waterfall here. The trail continues uphill, once again paralleling the clove. When the leaves are down, there are continuous views through the trees of Kaaterskill Clove and Kaaterskill High Peak.

**1.90** The trail makes a switchback to the right and begins to move away from Kaaterskill Clove. The Long Path now parallels the Escarpment Trail, which runs to the north, about 300 feet above the level of the Long Path. Again, there are views of Kaaterskill Clove through the trees, now with the Hudson River valley beyond.

**2.45** Reach a viewpoint to the east, down Kaaterskill Clove, with the Hudson Valley, the Hudson River and the Taconics visible beyond.

**2.65** The Long Path turns left, following the Sleepy Hollow Horse Trail, as another horse trail goes off to the right to the Palenville Lookout and Rip Van Winkle Hollow.

**2.85** Turn right onto the blue-blazed Escarpment Trail. (To the left, the Escarpment Trail leads to Inspiration Point and the Layman Monument).

**3.25** Reach the top of South Mountain. This was the site of the famous Hotel Kaaterskill, built in 1881 by George Harding, an influential guest at the Catskill Mountain House, who became upset when the Mountain House refused to accommodate the special dietary needs of his daughter. As a result, he left and built his own hotel (which was destroyed in a fire in 1924). The Long Path turns right, continuing along the blue-blazed Escarpment

Trail, as the red-blazed Schutt Road Trail goes off to the left. The Long Path now follows a wide and level trail.

**3.85** A red-blazed trail continues straight ahead and provides a shortcut to the Catskill Mountain House, as the Long Path turns right, following the blue-blazed Escarpment Trail, which begins to descend.

**4.05** Reach Split Rock and Boulder Rock, which afford a fine view of Kaaterskill Clove and the Hudson Valley. Boulder Rock—a large glacier erratic that is perched atop the ledge—makes a fine scramble for those who enjoy bouldering.

**4.15** The red-blazed shortcut trail rejoins from the left as the Long Path, still following the blue-blazed Escarpment Trail, continues north along the ledges. Soon the trail passes an area known as "Puddingstone Hall"—named for the conglomerate rock in the area—and descends to the Catskill Mountain House site.

**4.55** Reach the site of the former Catskill Mountain House. Built in 1824, it was the earliest and most famous of the old Catskill hotels, and was frequented by Presidents and famous artists. Just east of the hotel site, an inclined railway brought guests up from the Hudson Valley. The Mountain House fell into disrepair in the early twentieth century, when travellers chose the American West and Europe, rather than the Catskills, as the destinations for their summer vacations. It was burned in 1963 by the DEC, since it had become a hazard. The area around the hotel is well-worth exploring. From the hotel site, the trail continues along a former hotel access road towards North Lake and then turns right, along the Escarpment, and follows a chain-link fence.

**4.80** The trail passes through a picnic area, where a short side trail leads left to the North Lake parking lot (end of section). To continue, proceed straight ahead on the blue-blazed Escarpment Trail.

# Section 22

## North Lake to Batavia Kill

| Features | Catskill Escarpment, Blackhead Mountain |
|----------|------------------------------------------|

| Distance | 9.8 miles |
|----------|-----------|

### General description

This section of the Long Path offers dramatic scenery. From North Lake, the trail proceeds north along the Catskill Escarpment (also known as the "Great Wall of Manitou"), with many spectacular views of the Hudson River valley over 2,000 feet below. This area was made famous by Thomas Cole of the Hudson River School of Painting. After a steep climb to North Point, the trail becomes more rugged, descending from Stoppel Point to Dutcher Notch and then climbing Blackhead Mountain. The summit of Blackhead is the second highest point on the Long Path. North of Blackhead, the trail descends to the Batavia Kill Trail along one of the steepest trail sections in the Catskills. For the entire length of this section, the Long Path follows the Escarpment Trail, blazed with blue DEC trail markers.

### Access

Take the New York State Thruway to Exit 20 (Saugerties). Take Route 32 north to Route 32A. Continue on Route 32A north to Palenville. Turn left (west) onto Route 23A, and continue through Kaaterskill Clove to Haines Falls. In Haines Falls, turn right onto Greene

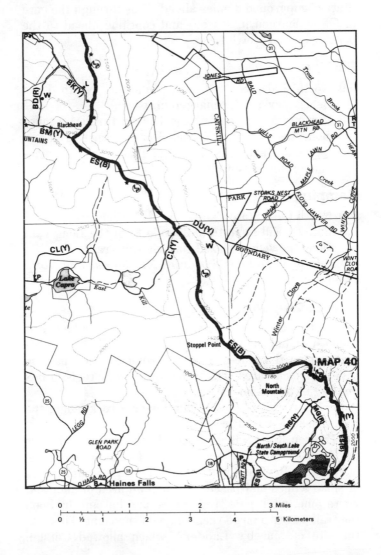

County Route 18 and follow the signs to North Lake State Campground 3 miles ahead. Pass through the gate (a fee is charged in season) and continue ahead to the parking area at North Lake.

## Parking

**0.0** North Lake State Campground, at North Lake Beach (parking fee charged in season).

**9.8** Parking area at end of Big Hollow Road (1.4 miles along the red-blazed Black Dome Range Trail and the yellow-blazed Batavia Kill Trail from the beginning of this section).

## Camping

**0.0** North Lake State Campground (fee charged).

**9.8** Batavia Kill Lean-to (0.25 mile from the Long Path along the yellow-blazed Batavia Kill Trail).

*Camping is prohibited between North Lake and North Point.*

## Trail description

**0.00** From the end of a short side trail which begins at the east end of the parking lot, the Long Path proceeds north along the blue-blazed Escarpment Trail, passing through a picnic area. The trail soon passes a register box and begins to ascend.

**0.30** After a short, steep climb over a rock ledge, the trail reaches Artist Rock, which provides a good view of the Hudson River valley. Artist Rock was made famous by Thomas Cole, the founder of the Hudson River School of Painting. Beyond Artist Rock, the trail climbs a series of small ledges and passes through an area of hemlock, white pine, pitch pine, red spruce and balsam fir. Soon the trail passes a large rock ledge on the right. This was the site of "Jacob's Ladder," which allowed Catskill

Mountain House visitors to climb up to Sunset Rock above.

**0.80**  To the right, a yellow-blazed side trail leads to the top of Sunset Rock, which offers a dramatic view of North and South Lakes and the site of the Catskill Mountain House, with Kaaterskill High Peak visible directly behind the lakes. This was the site of one of Thomas Cole's most famous paintings.

**1.00**  Reach Newman's Ledge, a large overhanging rock outcropping with a spectacular view north over the Hudson River valley. On a clear day, the tall buildings of Albany are visible in the distance, with the Taconics and Green Mountains of Vermont beyond. The trail now climbs about 140 feet and emerges in a open area, with an interesting mountaintop swamp which is well worth exploring.

**1.55**  The yellow-blazed Rock Shelter Trail leaves to the left. This trail drops into Mary's Glen and continues to the gatehouse at the entrance to the North Lake area. From Mary's Glen, the red-blazed Mary's Glen Trail can be followed back to North Lake. The Rock Shelter Trail is named for a large overhang known as Badman's Cave, which was reputed to be a hideout for outlaws in the 1700's. The Long Path continues to the right and climbs through a rocky area in a spruce-balsam forest.

**2.20**  The red-blazed Mary's Glen Trail leaves to the left. This trail descends through a beautiful wooded area and provides an alternate return route to North Lake. The Long Path continues ahead and begins a very steep ascent to North Point.

**2.35**  Reach North Point, an open rocky ledge, which provides a spectacular 360° view. To the south, directly below, are North and South Lakes, with Kaaterskill High Peak and Roundtop in the background. To the east is the ridge of the Escarpment that we have been following, with the Hudson Valley precipitously below. To the west

**North and South Lakes from North Point**

and immediately ahead is North Mountain, with Blackhead Mountain behind to the right (northwest). The City of Albany is visible in the distance to the northeast. From here the trail continues to climb North Mountain.

**2.80** Reach the summit of North Mountain (elevation 3,180 feet). While only slightly over 3,000 feet high, North Mountain has a spruce-balsam forest which is characteristic of the higher elevations. The trail continues up, at times steeply, through brushy, rocky areas.

**4.05** Reach Stoppel Point (elevation 3,420 feet), which provides a view northeast over the Hudson Valley, with Albany and the Taconics in the distance. Stoppel Point was the site of a recent plane crash, and parts of the wreckage may still be seen. From Stoppel Point, the trail begins to descend towards Dutcher Notch, with occasional views of the Blackhead Range through the trees. The trail soon levels off.

**5.15** The trail curves to the north and soon resumes its descent. Just before the descent, there is an excellent view back to the southeast. From here, it is evident that you have already descended a substantial distance from Stoppel Point. After a short, steep descent, the trail levels off again.

**6.30** After another short, steep descent, the trail reaches Dutcher Notch (elevation 2,500 feet), the lowest point on the Escarpment Trail since just beyond North Lake. To the right, the yellow-blazed Dutcher Notch Trail drops 1,700 feet in 2.4 miles to Floyd Hawver Road. There is a reliable spring on the Dutcher Notch Trail 0.35 mile and about 500 vertical feet below this point—the only reliable *water* in this section. To the left, the yellow-blazed Colgate Lake Trail descends to Colgate Lake, first passing around an unnamed lake and skirting private Lake Capra. The Long Path continues straight ahead, beginning a steep ascent to a level plateau sometimes known as Arizona.

**7.15** After an 800-foot climb, the trail reaches the Arizona plateau and begins to level off. To the left, a short side trail leads to a viewpoint back towards Stoppel Point and Lakes Capra and Colgate. The trail follows this level plateau for about a mile, with increasingly spectacular views of Blackhead Mountain straight ahead.

**8.30** The trail begins its final 600-foot ascent to the summit of Blackhead Mountain. Near the summit, there is a spectacular view to the east over the Escarpment below, with Albany and the Taconics visible to the north.

**8.80** Reach the summit of Blackhead Mountain (elevation 3,940 feet), the second highest point on the Long Path and the fourth highest mountain in the Catskills. The view from the summit is overgrown, but views to the south are possible by heading into the scrub vegetation just left of the trail. Here, the Long Path, following the blue-blazed Escarpment Trail, turns right, as the yellow-blazed Blackhead Mountain Trail goes straight ahead and descends to Lockwood Gap between Blackhead and Black Dome Mountains. (It is worth the 0.2-mile detour down this trail to a spectacular view to the south and west). The Long Path soon drops precipitously down the north face of Blackhead, plunging over ledges in one of the steepest descents in the Catskills. Near the base of the descent, there are two fine views of the Hudson Valley to the east.

**9.80** Reach the base of the descent from Blackhead Mountain (end of section). Here, the yellow-blazed Batavia Kill Trail descends to the left, passing the Batavia Kill Lean-to in 0.25 mile, and ending at the red-blazed Black Dome Range Trail in 0.9 mile. (From this point, the Black Dome Range Trail continues straight ahead to the parking area at the end of Big Hollow Road in another 0.5 mile). To continue on the Long Path, proceed straight ahead on the blue-blazed Escarpment Trail.

**Black Dome from Blackhead Mountain**

# Section 23

*Batavia Kill to Route 23 (East Windham)*

---

**Features**   *Northern Catskill Escarpment,*
*Windham High Peak*

---

**Distance**                    *8.55 miles*

---

## General description

The Long Path continues along the blue-blazed Escarpment Trail to Route 23 in East Windham. The trail crosses several 3,000-foot peaks before making the final climb over Windham High Peak. There are many views along the way over the Blackhead Range to the south and the Catskill and Mohawk valleys to the north. On a clear day, one can see all the way to the southern Adirondacks. From Windham High Peak, the trail descends to Route 23, at the northern edge of the Catskill Park, passing through two groves of Norway spruce planted by the CCC in the 1930's. For the entire length of this section, the Long Path follows the Escarpment Trail, blazed with blue DEC trail markers.

## Access

Take the New York State Thruway to Exit 21 (Catskill). Continue on Route 23 west about 22 miles to Brooksburg. At a sign for Hensonville, turn left and proceed south on County Route 65. In Hensonville, turn left onto County Route 40 and follow it to Maplecrest. In Maplecrest, bear left onto Big Hollow Road, passing the Sugar Maples Resort, and continue about 5 miles to a parking area at the end of the road. To reach the beginning of this section of the Long Path, follow the red-blazed Black Dome Range Trail straight ahead for 0.5 mile to the intersection with the yellow-blazed Batavia Kill Trail. Continue ahead on the Batavia Kill Trail 0.9 mile to the Escarpment Trail.

## Parking

**0.0** Parking area at end of Big Hollow Road (1.4 miles along the red-blazed Black Dome Range Trail and the yellow-blazed Batavia Kill Trail from the beginning of this section).

**8.5** Parking area on Route 23 in East Windham, at intersection with Cross Road.

## Camping

**0.0** Batavia Kill Lean-to (0.25 mile from the Long Path along the yellow-blazed Batavia Kill Trail).

**7.4** Elm Ridge Lean-to.

## Trail description

**0.00** From the intersection of the blue-blazed Escarpment Trail with the yellow-blazed Batavia Kill trail, the Long Path proceeds north along the Escarpment Trail, soon ascending an unnamed knob, with a fine viewpoint over the Hudson Valley. Although the trail runs close to the edge of the Escarpment, there are no other views on this section of the trail. The trail soon begins a gradual climb up to Acra Point.

**1.80** Reach the open rock summit of Acra Point (elevation 3,100 feet). The view here is somewhat obscured by low growth. However, a short distance down the trail there is an open view to the west towards Big Hollow, with the Blackhead Range towering behind. As the trail begins to descend, a short side trail to the left leads to an open rock with another view toward Big Hollow and the

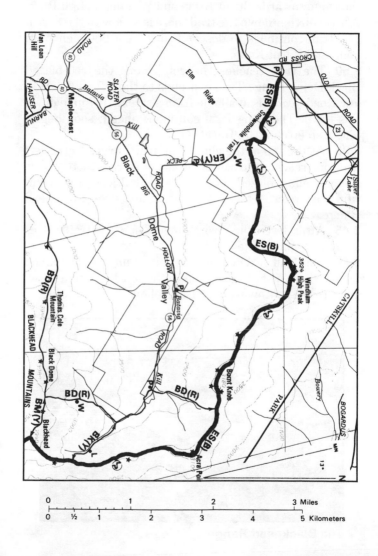

Blackhead Range. There is also a view northwest along the ridge towards Burnt Knob and Windham High Peak. A little further down the trail there is a view to the north. The trail continues to descend to the col between Acra Point and Burnt Knob.

**2.50** The trail reaches the col, where the red-blazed Black Dome Range Trail descends to the left to Big Hollow Road (*water* is available from a stream 0.7 mile down this trail). The Long Path continues ahead, soon beginning a steep climb up Burnt Knob.

**2.80** At the top of the climb, the trail curves to the left and soon reaches the southern side of Burnt Knob, where a short yellow-blazed side trail to the left leads to a beautiful viewpoint over Big Hollow and the Blackhead Range.

**3.45** After descending from Burnt Knob, the trail passes by a viewpoint to the north.

**3.80** The trail reaches the summit of another unnamed knob, where a short side trail to the left leads to a viewpoint to the southwest over Big Hollow.

**The Blackhead Range**

**View from Windham High Peak**

**3.95** After descending from the knob, the trail begins its ascent of Windham High Peak.

**4.35** The trail passes through an open area, with views of Windham High Peak directly ahead, and soon begins to ascend steadily.

**5.05** The Trail reaches the summit of Windham High Peak (elevation 3,524 feet). Just before the summit, there is a large rock outcropping to the right, with an open view to the north. Sometimes called the "Great Northern Viewpoint," this is the last spectacular view from the Escarpment Trail. To the north, the lesser peaks of Ginseng, Hayden, Pisgah and Huntersfield—followed by the Long Path to the north—are visible. In the far distance, the Helderbergs and the southern Adirondacks may be seen on a clear day. The Hudson River valley is visible to the northeast and, on a clear day, the City of Albany, the Taconics and the Green Mountains of Vermont may also be seen. The trail bears left and continues along the level summit, with a partial view over the Blackhead Range to the southeast, and another partial view northwest at the west end of the summit, then begins a steady descent.

**6.75** The trail enters the first of two groves of Norway spruce trees planted by the Civilian Conservation Corps in the 1930's. The trail climbs over the tangled roots of these trees. Between the two groves, the trail passes through a small open area.

**7.40** Shortly after passing a short yellow-blazed side trail to a rock ledge (the view from this point is obscured by overgrown vegetation), the trail passes the Elm Ridge Lean-to, to the left of the trail.

**7.45** The Long Path turns right at a junction, continuing along the blue-blazed Escarpment Trail, as the yellow-blazed Elm Ridge Trail descends to the left for 0.85 mile to the parking area at the end of Peck Road. The Long Path now follows a wide snowmobile trail—the route of an old turnpike across the mountains.

**7.60** Turn left, leaving the old road, and continue to descend on a narrower path.

**7.70** Turn sharply to the right and descend steeply.

**8.55** After passing a trail register, the trail crosses a bridge over a stream and reaches Route 23 near East Windham (end of section). To continue, go across Route 23 and follow Cross Road to the northwest.

**Escarpment Trail at Route 23**

# Section 24

*Route 23 (East Windham) to
Greene County Route 10*

| | |
|---|---|
| ***Features*** | *Ginseng Mountain,*<br>*Mt. Hayden* |
| ***Distance*** | *6.95 miles* |

### General description

In this section, the Long Path leaves the Catskill Park—after a journey of 94 miles—and continues to the north. The terrain is similar to that found in Catskills, but on a smaller scale. The primary ridge followed by the trail in this section is a continuation of the Catskill Escarpment. For much of the distance along the ridge, the trail follows logging roads. The area is still alive with logging activity, but forest recovers quickly, as there has not been any clear cutting. There are no great open views, but there are many good views along the way when the leaves are down. The trail crosses two notches, Jenne and Barlow, which are bisected by the remnants of old mountain turnpikes that connected the mountains to the valley to the east. The first 0.75 mile of the section goes through state land and is marked with blue DEC trail markers, while the rest of the section is on private land and is marked with aqua Long Path paint blazes. On these private lands, crossed with the permission of the owners, no camping and no fires of any kind are permitted. This section of the trail is closed during deer hunting season.

## Access

Take the New York State Thruway to Exit 21 (Catskill). Continue on Route 23 west approximately 20 miles to East Windham. About 0.5 mile past the "Entering Catskill Park" sign, turn right at Cross Road. There is a DEC parking area just south of the intersection of Route 23 and Cross Road.

## Parking

**0.0** Parking area on Route 23 in East Windham, at intersection with Cross Road.

**6.3** Intersection of Sutton Road and Cunningham Road.

**6.9** Greene County Route 10.

## Trail description

**0.00** From the intersection of Route 23 and Cross Road, proceed north on Cross Road for about 150 feet—just beyond the DEC parking area. The Long Path (blazed with blue DEC trail markers) then turns right, crosses a small field and enters the woods. The trail continues east, parallel to Route 23, crosses a stone wall, passes through a swampy area and then crosses another stone wall.

**0.30** Here we leave the Catskill Park, which the Long Path has traversed for the last 94 miles. The trail turns left, away from Route 23, and ascends gradually to an old spruce and hemlock forest. From here, the trail descends gradually to the left.

**0.75** Cross Old Road and continue north on paved Jenne Notch Road. The Long Path now leaves state land, and for the remainder of the section it is marked with aqua paint blazes. Jenne Notch Road soon becomes a gravel road.

**1.30** After passing several houses, Jenne Notch Road officially ends at an old red brick house. The trail passes through an iron gate and continues along a newly-

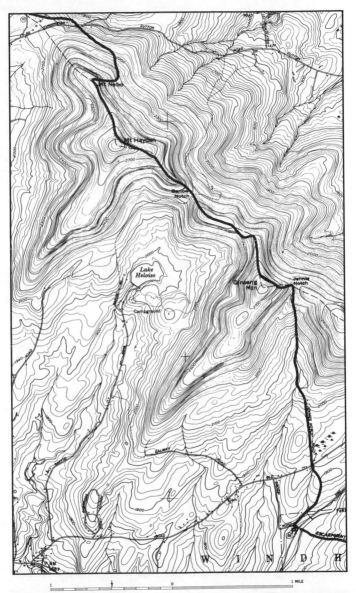

constructed gravel road uphill to Jenne Notch. This road follows the route of an old 19th century mountain turnpike.

**2.35** At the height of land, the trail turns sharply to the left and begins a steep climb up Ginseng Mountain on an old logging road. At the top of the steep rise, the trail turns right, leaving the logging road, and proceeds through a logged area. (Much of the ridgetop that the trail follows from here to Mt. Hayden is still used today for forestry and logging). The trail goes to the east of and below the summit of Ginseng Mountain, and it soon emerges on an old logging road just north of the summit.

**2.85** The trail turns onto a newer logging road and descends to the north off Ginseng Mountain. Along this section, there are good views ahead to Mt. Hayden on the ridge and to Mt. Pisgah and Huntersfield Mountain in the distance. Huntersfield Mountain (elevation 3,423 feet) is the highest mountain in the Catskills north of Route 23.

**3.20** The logging road which has been followed by the trail turns left and descends steeply to Lake Heloise (where there is a private campground) as the Long Path continues ahead along the western edge of the ridge, skirting a recently logged area. There are views back towards Ginseng Mountain to the south, and west through the trees to Lake Heloise and Cave Mountain, home of the Windham Ski Resort. Soon the trail turns back toward the center of the ridge. It then turns very sharply left and climbs an unnamed knob.

**3.70** Reach the top of the knob, which is grassy and logged. The trail now descends, first to the west and then to the north, towards Barlow Notch.

**4.00** Reach Barlow Notch. Here the trail crosses another old mountain turnpike, joins a logging road and ascends the southeast slopes of Mt. Hayden. As you climb, you can look back along the ridge to Ginseng Mountain and Windham High Peak in the distance. The trail alternates between steep sections and level stretches.

**4.75** Leave the logging road and continue along a foot-path towards the summit of Mt. Hayden.

**4.95** Reach the level summit of Mt. Hayden (elevation 2,920 feet), which is the highest point on this section of the Long Path. From here, the trail descends steeply at first and then more gradually to the col between Mt. Hayden and Mt. Nebo, following a faint old road for most of this section. Just beyond the col, the trail crosses to the east side of the ridge and begins to a short, gradual ascent of Mt. Nebo (which is really a spur of Mt. Hayden).

**5.55** Reach the summit of Mt. Nebo. Here the trail turns right and descends to the east, gradually at first and then steeply via a series of switchbacks, with views through the trees to the farms and fields of the Hudson Valley below. At the bottom of the steep section, the trail joins an old road that parallels the ridge and descends to an open field with an abandoned house and then to Sutton Road.

**6.30** Turn left onto Sutton Road, and soon reach an intersection with Cunningham Road. Here the trail turns right and re-enters the woods. The trail continues westward, parallel to Cunningham Road, descending gradually.

**6.95** After a brief climb, reach Greene County Route 10 (end of section). To continue, cross Route 10 and proceed uphill on a quarry road.

# Section 25

*Greene County Route 10 to
Greene County Route 32C*

| | |
|---|---|
| ***Features*** | *Mt. Pisgah, Richtmyer Peak,
Richmond Mountain* |

| | |
|---|---|
| ***Distance*** | *4.5 miles* |

### General description

After a short section on private land, this section of the Long Path enters the first of many state reforestation areas between the Catskills and the Mohawk River. The trail climbs steeply up Mt. Pisgah and follows the ridgetop for the rest of the way, passing through both mixed deciduous forests and plantations of red pine and Norway spruce. There are several good views, both north towards the southern Adirondacks, and south towards the Blackhead Range and the Devil's Path. The Long Path currently ends at Greene County Route 32C on the Greene/Schoharie county line, but work continues to extend it further north. The first 0.55 mile of the section goes through private land and is marked with aqua Long Path paint blazes, while the rest of the section is on state land and is blazed with blue DEC trail markers.

### Access

Take the New York State Thruway to Exit 21 (Catskill). Continue on Route 23 west approximately 20 miles to the Town of Windham. In Windham, turn right on Mitchell Hollow Road and go north about 5 miles to Greene Coun-

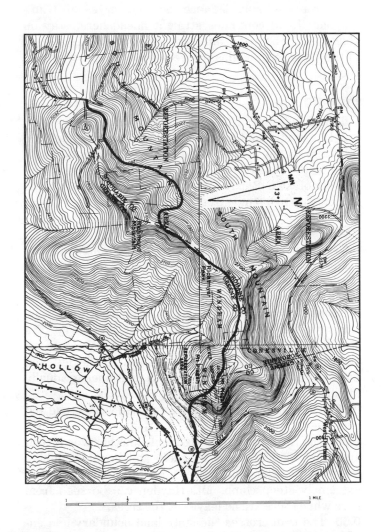

ty Route 10. Turn right on Route 10, which continues east for a very short distance and then curves left (Cunningham Road continues straight ahead here; stay on Route 10). About 0.3 mile past the curve, this section of the Long Path begins where a woods road goes off to the left.

## Parking

**0.0** Greene County Route 10 at the trailhead.

**4.2** Intersection of CCC Road and woods road on left.

**4.5** Intersection of CCC Road and Greene County Route 32C (there is room to park several cars on the shoulder of CCC Road). (In winter, Route 32C is plowed only up to 0.3 mile from the trailhead).

## Trail description

**0.00** From Greene County Route 10, the Long Path proceeds uphill on a quarry road (blocked by a metal chain to prevent vehicle access). The trail—marked with aqua paint blazes—follows the quarry road for about 250 feet, turns left and passes through a red pine plantation, then turns right and skirts the south side of the quarry. The trail soon reaches a interesting rock wall, follows it to the right, then makes a sharp switchback to the left and passes through a cleft in the cliff. It continues gradually uphill through the woods.

**0.25** The trail turns right onto an eroded woods road and continues uphill.

**0.35** The Long Path turns right onto another woods road and then immediately turns left and begins climbing steeply. Soon the trail crosses a rock wall and begins an extremely steep climb. Mt. Hayden can be seen from here when there are no leaves on the trees.

**0.55** The trail crosses the state land boundary and enters the Mt. Pisgah Reforestation Area. The trail blazing now changes to blue DEC trail markers. The trail continues uphill, intersects a woods road and finally turns left for the final ascent to the summit of Mt. Pisgah.

**0.85** Reach the summit of Mt. Pisgah (elevation 2,912 feet). This was formerly the site of a summit observatory (remnants of the well that supplied water to the site may still be seen). To the south is the old carriage road that provided access from the valley. The summit was once cleared of vegetation, but today it is covered with a mature Norway spruce and red pine grove. There is a view to the north of the Helderbergs and the Adirondacks in the distance. From the summit, the Long Path descends through the forest. It soon approaches the state land boundary, where it turns left and continues to descend on state land. There is an interesting contrast here between the deep greens of the spruce and pine grove and the lighter greens of the deciduous forest to the right. After a while, the trail leaves the evergreen grove and continues to descend.

**1.25** Reach the col between Mt. Pisgah and Richtmyer Peak. The trail now begins a gradual ascent, skirting below private land to the north. Soon it turns right, ascends to the top of the ridge and then turns left to follow the ridge. After a level stretch, the trail continues to ascend to Richtmyer Peak.

**2.20** The Long Path reaches the flat summit of Richtmyer Peak (elevation 2,980 feet). To the left, there is a seasonal view through the trees towards the Blackhead Range. The trail then turns right and makes a very short descent to the col between Richtmyer Peak and Richmond Mountain. The trail continues along the ridge and climbs to the east summit of Richmond Mountain.

**2.60** Reach the east summit of Richmond Mountain (elevation 3,120 feet). To the left, a short side trail leads to a view to the south, with the Blackhead Range, Kaaterskill

High Peak and the Devil's Path visible. The Long Path continues along the ridge and descends to the col between the two peaks of Richmond Mountain. Here it levels off and follows the north shoulder of the main peak of Richmond Mountain, avoiding private land, then begins a steep descent.

**3.35** Turn right, onto a woods road, and continue to descend. Soon another woods road joins from the right. The trail continues ahead to the left.

**3.50** The trail levels off and turns left onto another woods road (which was recently used by the state to log adjacent lands).

**4.20** Turn right onto CCC Road, a dirt road marked as a state motor vehicle trail, and descend gradually.

**4.50** Reach an intersection with Greene County Route 32C (end of section). To the left, Route 32C descends to Windham. To the right, CCC Road leads to Conesville in Schoharie County. The Long Path presently ends here, but will be extended north along the ridge.

**Painted Trillium**